Praise for

IDENTITY THEFT

Read *Identity Theft* and you will make two discoveries: it's just about impossible not to like Mike, and just about unfathomable not to be grateful for the person God made you to be.

JOHN ORTBERG, Pastor,
Menlo Park Presbyterian Church and Author,
When the Game Is Over, It All Goes Back in the Box

I can't imagine anything more significant in our image-crazed culture than grounding our identity in the right place. With biblical wisdom, humor, and raw honesty, the author gives us tools for the battle to see ourselves accurately, from God's perspective instead of our own distorted mirrors. Mike, thank you for the gift of this book!

NANCY BEACH,
Teaching Pastor and Champion for the Arts,
Willow Creek Association

So many people today desperately need to hear
what Mike is saying within these pages.
I know I did! We are far too often robbed by the
false thinking that our culture subtly teaches us.
Mike clears that up for us and gives us hope
for seeing ourselves as God does.

DAN KIMBALL, Pastor,
Vintage Faith Church and Author,
They Like Jesus but Not the Church

Our generation gets bombarded
with mixed messages: "Buy this," "Look like that,"
"Achieve more," if you want to be somebody.
Mike Breaux cuts through the confusion
with clarity and humor, pointing us back
to the life-giving Source of a truly secure I.D.
A must-read for anyone who has ever wondered,
"Who did God intend me to be?"

JOHN BURKE, Pastor,
Gateway Community Church and Author,
No Perfect People Allowed

IDENTITY

THEFT

ALSO BY MIKE BREAUX

Making Ripples

IDENTITY THEFT

Reclaiming Who God Created You to Be

MIKE BREAUX

ZONDERVAN®

WILLOW
Willow Creek Resources

ZONDERVAN.com/
AUTHORTRACKER
follow your favorite authors

Identity Theft
Copyright © 2007 by Mike Breaux

Requests for information should be addressed to:
Zondervan, *Grand Rapids, Michigan* 49530

Library of Congress Cataloging-in-Publication Data

Breaux, Mike.
     Identity theft : reclaiming who God created you to be / Mike Breaux.
        p.   cm.
     Includes bibliographical references.
     ISBN-10: 0-310-27765-5
     ISBN-13: 978-0-310-27765-1
     1. Identification (Religion) 2. Self-actualization (Psychology) — Religious
aspects — Christianity. I. Title.
     BV4509.5.B73   2007
     248.4 — dc22
                                                2007011547

This edition printed on acid-free paper.

Interior design by Beth Shagene

Printed in the United States of America

07 08 09 10 11 12 13 • 20 19 18 17 16 15 14 13 12 11 10 9 8 7 6 5 4 3 2 1

For Jodi and Mike, Derrick and Lauren,
Drew and Laura,
treasured children of the Most High God

CONTENTS

ACKNOWLEDGMENTS

I was so grateful to graduate from college knowing I'd never have to write a ten-page research paper ever again. But that's pretty much all I've been doing since I got out! Having the privilege and responsibility to research, create, and write messages that just might help move people closer to God has been a blast—a daunting blast because talking on behalf of God is pretty scary.

Actually, I've enjoyed writing ever since I published my first high school essay, "What I Did on My First Date" (currently out of print). However, as much as I like to write, it's a lot easier for me to get up and talk than it is to sit down and type. Writing something for people to read is far different than writing something for people to listen to in church. It's a challenge for me. So I'm grateful to people like Christine Anderson and Judy Keene for the excellence they bring to this craft. They are incredibly patient and good. In fact, I hope they edit this page for me too.

Partnering with John Raymond and the wonderful team at Zondervan is an honor. I still can't believe I'm a published author!

The people I work with at Willow Creek Community Church and the Willow Creek Association—Bill, Gene, Tammy, Randy, Jon, Greg, Brian, Nancy, Jimmy, and the rest of the team—inspire me and pour into my life more than they will ever know. I am especially grateful for the brainstorming team of Leanne, Randy, Chris, Jeff, and Emily. It was so fun, wasn't it guys?

"Thanks" seems an inadequate word for the person who keeps my life organized, but thanks so much, Marge!

Good friends like Gordon and Ross hold me accountable to being who God made me to be and living strong for him. Thanks for your honesty and the strokes you give me on each nine.

Debbie, as my buddies say, "Bro, you sure out-kicked your punt coverage when you married her." I don't know what that means exactly, but I know I'm in way over my head. Everyone knows it! I'm blessed.

Our whole family is blessed. We go on vacation—all twenty of us—every year and stay in the same house and never get tired of each other. Well, they might get tired of me, but I'd rather hang out with Shirley, Molly, Dave, Kris, Casey, Courtney, Courtney, Danny, and all my kids than anyone else!

Lastly, to Hayden and Bryce ... you're what I hope to be when I grow up.

Thanks, God, for your high, wide, long, and deep love.

Mike

ROLL CALL

I always hated the first day of school. Not because it announced the end of summer and the beginning of a yearlong diet of cafeteria soybean burgers. Not because I had a fear of big yellow buses or big-haired librarians. I hated the first day of school because of my name.

Ever know anyone with a name that just got massacred during every first-day-of-school roll call? My name (as any good Cajun would know) is pronounced "Bro," with a long *o*. It is, however, spelled "Breaux." My parents named me Mike and everybody calls me Mike, which is an abbreviated version of my *middle* name, Michael. But my first name is actually Jerry. So on opening day in every class from kindergarten to graduate school, I heard, "Jerry *Bree-ox?*"

I would raise my hand and say, "Mike *Bro.*"

"No, wait your turn, please. I'm looking for Jerry *Bree-ox*." It drove me crazy!

This went on for seventeen years of school—and it still happens to me far more often than you might imagine. "*Bree-ox*, party of four?" "Jerry *Bree-ox*, the doctor will see you now." "Mr. *Bree-ox*? Your car is ready." Do you get the picture? It's a good thing *I* know who I am.

And in fact, that knowledge has made me quite passionate about writing this book, because way too many people really *don't* know who they are. Oh, they've got a first and last name. They probably have a Social Security number or a student ID card. Maybe they even have a title. But the fact is, they're pretty clueless when it comes to their true identity.

I hear from these folks all the time. Sometimes they send me emails or handwritten notes detailing their confusion, a few of which I have permission to share with you in the pages ahead. Some of them approach me after a service at our church, often choking back tears because something from the message has exposed a crack in their fragile identity. At other times, I sit across the table from a person in enormous pain who is spilling out the disastrous results of pretending to be someone God never intended him or her to be. And then, of course, there are the celebrations when the holes in people's hearts are filled up and their anxiety relieved, as they recognize and claim the authentic reality of who they really are. How about you—do you know who *you* are? If someone were to ask, "Who are you, anyway?" what would you say?

Most of us might respond to such a question with answers that describe what we do, where we're from, who we hang with, what we look like, or any number of other descriptors. For instance, I might answer the question by saying I'm a pastor, I'm from Kentucky, I'm married to Debbie and the dad of three kids. I drive a truck, have a really cool dog and a really ugly golf swing. Our unique, individual descriptors are what make us all so interesting, don't you think?

> How about you —
> do you know who *you* are?
> If someone were to ask,
> "Who are you, anyway?"
> what would you say?

Way too often, though, our descriptors end up laying claim to far more of our lives than they deserve—so much so, they actually become who we *are*. This misappropriation is a recipe for disaster, because it has the power to steal away our very identities. And while there are various ways for identity theft to happen, I've learned—from personal experience and through my conversations with hundreds of victims—that four situations are especially problematic.

These include the pursuit of *relationships*, where someone else's view of who a person should be totally eclipses who the person actually is. Take the man or woman who obliterates his or her true self in order to create an identity acceptable to a person who might love them. Or the teenager desperate for acceptance who does things contrary to his or her own convictions in order to fit into the crowd. Who is that person, exactly, when the lover or the crowd goes away?

Others among us build our identities around *appearance*, convinced that if we can only be thinner, fitter, handsomer, blonder, curlier, more muscular, prettier, or some other modification of what we look like, our craving for acceptance will be satisfied. Now, we all enjoy looking our best—and we need to properly care for the bodies God has entrusted to us. But when our appearance becomes our identity, we are in danger of succumbing to problems ranging from eating disorders to insecurity-driven physical alterations.

Another area with the power to steal our identity is *success*. Like relationships and appearance, success in itself is an attribute—God gave us the motivation to achieve and the encouragement to make the most of our lives. But when the all-consuming pursuit of the corner office, the trophy, or the applause becomes our identity, it can and does wreck lives, relationships, and even our very souls. "And how do you benefit if you gain the whole world but lose your own soul?" asked Jesus nearly two thousand years ago (Matt. 16:26). Talk about a culturally relevant question.

And then there is what may be the thorniest issue of all, a person's *past.* For some of us, the belittling or hurtful parental judgments hammered into us as children continue to play again and again in our adult minds. For others, our own past behaviors result in shame or guilt, creating an identity that can entrap us long after those behaviors have ceased. In both cases, the past distorts our self-image, substituting a false identity for the one we were meant to enjoy.

The good news is that none of this is a surprise to God. In his love for us, he has offered the very remedy we need to foil the theft and reclaim the identities he meant for each of us to have in the first place.

In the pages ahead, you'll learn more about each of these four variations of identity theft, in many cases directly from women and men who, once they realized their identities had been stolen, stepped up to take them back and now live in truth and authenticity. More importantly, you'll learn about the remedy. My prayer is that if your identity has been stolen—or if that has been the case with someone you know or love—that this book may serve as a key to help unlock the freedom that accompanies authentic identity.

> In his love for us,
> he has offered the very remedy
> we need to foil the theft
> and reclaim the identities
> he meant for each of us to have
> in the first place.

I hope you'll enjoy reading, and maybe even laugh a time or two, but that in the end you will recognize the powerful truth of God's unfailing love. And that where there was once theft and loss, there will be restoration and health. Because for you to discover who you really are would make Jerry *Bree-ox* really, really happy.

1

ROBBED BY RELATIONSHIPS

have kept this little toy in my office for more than fifteen years now — up on the shelf right between the Etch A Sketch and my Las Vegas Hilton ashtray. The toy belonged to my son Drew, and if you've been a child or a parent in the last thirty years, you may have owned one too.

Officially known as a Shape-O Toy, you probably called it the Tupperware ball. One half of the plastic globe is red, the other half is blue. And the toy includes ten holes, each one sized to correspond with a yellow plastic star, triangle, or other shape. Those shapes stay inside the ball until someone pulls it apart to release the pieces, and then tries to match them up with the correctly shaped hole until they're all back inside the ball. (Since I'm from Kentucky, this was actually my ACT test. Just kidding!)

When Drew was four years old, he would get so frustrated playing with this toy. He'd try to force the piece in his hand into the particular hole he wanted it to go into. We'd hear him back in his room just grunting and banging away on the toy. Then he'd come walking down the hall, and I'd ask him, "Hey, Drew, where ya going?"

"Gonna get a hammer," he'd answer. Then he'd come back and whack on that ball some more. He got so ticked off at that plastic puzzle-toy!

I've kept that Tupperware ball in my office over the years, not so much to remember my son's frustration with his toy, but to remind me that millions and millions of people are equally frustrated with life. Every time I see it sitting there on the shelf by the window, it renews my passion and reminds me why I do what I do. Because it breaks my heart to look around our culture and see so many people trying to cram square pegs into the round holes of their lives—all in an effort to find satisfaction, to find purpose ... to find their identities.

That search is nothing new, of course. Take a guy named Solomon, the richest man who ever lived—so rich he makes Bill Gates look like, well, *me*. He had every resource available to him as he

searched to "find himself" and to determine what
would fit the hole in the human heart. You ought to
read his very honest journal, the book of Ecclesiastes
in the Bible, where he describes all the square pegs
he used to try and fill up the gaping round hole in
his heart.

He attempted, as he puts it, "everything under
the sun" to find the perfect fit, to see what would
fill that void. He tried massive real estate ventures.
He built incredible mansions, palaces, gardens,
parks, and reservoirs. He got into music and art. He
experimented with unbridled sexual encounters.
He overdosed on choice food, vintage wine, and
the biggest, wildest parties anyone could throw.
But at the end of his life, he said, "You
know what I've discovered? It's all
meaningless. It's just like chasing
after the wind." It was like trying
to cram a square peg into a round
hole.

You see, deep within our hearts
is a God-shaped hole, and trying to fill it with
anything else just doesn't work.

Solomon continued his pursuit. And then later,
in the book of Proverbs, he writes a concluding
thought: "What a person desires is unfailing love"
(Prov. 19:22 TNIV). And don't you sense that
is true? Don't you agree that the thing we're all

seeking is an unfailing love to fill up the hole in our heart?

So we go looking for that kind of love—too often in all the wrong places. Our culture revolves around that quest. Bookstore shelves sag beneath the weight of volumes of romance novels. Hollywood studios crank out love story after love story. And how many love songs does late-night radio host Delilah send out over the airwaves every evening for all those listeners yearning for that elusive unfailing love?

You see, deep within our hearts
is a God-shaped hole,
and trying to fill it
with anything else just doesn't work.

Singers pledge passionate devotion with lyrics like, "Ain't no mountain high enough. Ain't no valley low enough. Ain't no river wide enough to keep me away from you." (I'm thinking, "What you need is a *restraining* order on this person!")

The movies are equally pathetic. I was flipping cable channels the other night and there it was again. It's on all the time—that movie starring Tom Cruise as sports agent Jerry Maguire. Do you remember the three famous lines from that movie? The most well-known one, of course, has got to be

"Show me the money!" Then there's the one uttered by Jerry's wife Dorothy (Renee Zellweger), who purrs, "You had me at hello." But the line that just kills me is when Jerry gives his wife this "I'm-sorry-for-all-the-pain-I've-caused-you" look and says, "You complete me." You *complete* me. Makes me want to puke!

My wife Debbie and I have been married for twenty-nine years now. For the five years we dated before that, our theme song was, "I love you more today than yesterday, but not as much as tomorrow." I'd crank it up on the radio and call her up just to play that song to her over the phone. Then we'd just kind of breathe at each other for a long time. (Oh, you've done it too!) But it was our song, our love song. And these days when it plays on an oldies station, it still makes us smile.

And you know what? It's true about us. I really do love her more today than yesterday, and I fully expect to love her even more tomorrow. It grows every day for me, and she is my soul mate. She's my best friend. I would rather hang out with Debbie than anybody else on the planet. I miss her when I'm traveling, and at the end of each day, I can't wait to just go home and be with her. But make no mistake about it: she does not *complete* me. And I know this is going to come as a shock to you, but she would tell you I don't complete her either.

Do you remember what Solomon said? "What a person desires is *unfailing* love." Only that kind of love can fill up the hole in your heart. To hope for another imperfect human being to provide that for you is to set yourself up for huge disappointment. To expect a human relationship to complete you is to embark on a long, uphill struggle, because such expectations are both unfair and unrealistic.

They can also be dangerous. For in our desperation to become a person who can attract and hold onto the unfailing love and completion we're longing for, way too many of us sacrifice who we really are. We give up our very identity.

> To expect a human relationship
> to complete you is to embark
> on a long, uphill struggle,
> because such expectations are
> both unfair and unrealistic.

WHO'S LIVING YOUR LIFE?

A recent *Newsweek* cover story detailed "The Scary New World of Identity Theft." One of the stories the article told was of a twenty-three-year-old single mom from Atlanta whose identity was stolen. She discovered that a former coworker opened more than twenty-five credit card accounts, took out loans, and even applied for a marriage license in her name! Her ex-colleague allegedly ran up $37,000 in charges, including the purchase of a car, leading the victim to tell *Newsweek*, "It's really scary knowing that someone else has been living my life."*

It is scary, isn't it, to think that somebody else could take over your identity like that? But tragically, I see it all the time. I see people allowing others to live their lives for them. I watch high school students do just about anything and morph into just about anyone they need to be in order to be accepted by a certain group, a certain guy, or a certain girl. Why do you think gangs flourish? Why do you think people so readily give up their bodies sexually? It's because they need to be accepted by an unfailing love. That desire is so strong that we are willing to be whoever we need to be—and in the process, we allow other people to live our lives.

Why do men and women compromise their values at work? Why do we care so much about what other people think or say about us? Why do we end up in codependent patterns and relationships out of our desire to be needed? It's because we're craving acceptance and significance in our lives. So we

---

* Steven Levy and Brad Stone, "The Scary New World of Identity Theft," *Newsweek*, July 4, 2005, 41.

devote ourselves to cramming the square shape of relationships with imperfect people into that round hole in our heart. And in the process, our identity is stolen.

Anyone who lives that way long enough is going to get really, really hurt somewhere along the line. Hasn't that been true in your experience? Haven't you found that people eventually disappoint you? Even as healthy and as good as relationships can be, they don't possess an *unfailing* love. People will break promises. People will betray you. People will exclude you. They'll reject you and wound you. They'll embarrass you, use you, and even abuse you. No excuses, but that's just part of being imperfect. And when you get stung by one of those imperfect people—especially someone you were expecting to *complete* you—all that acceptance and security and significance you've been counting on is gone. And your identity is gone with it.

The Bible says that if you're not careful, this hurt, disillusionment, and disappointment from a stolen identity can turn you into a totally different person. You may know what I'm talking about. When you're hurt in a relationship, when the unfailing love you desired bails on you, a wave of bitterness can wash into the void. And when that bitterness takes over, watch out. When resentment rolls around inside you, you begin to turn into an angry, distant,

cynical, oversensitive, ticked-off-at-the-world kind
of person. You become withdrawn. You become
selfish. You become self-absorbed. You grow
distant. You're distrustful and even a bit paranoid.
When bitterness hacks into your life, it really messes
you up.

Look at what the Bible says: "Resentment kills
a fool, and envy slays the simple" (Job 5:2 NIV).
Resentment kills a fool—or, as one of Job's friends
reminded him, "You are only hurting yourself with
your anger" (Job 18:4 GN).

Man, that's so true. I've been there. I've been in
that place where I've thought I was sticking it to
that dirty, rotten scoundrel who hurt me—only
to discover that, in reality, I was using my anger
to stick it to *myself*. I once went a whole year not
speaking to a coach who cut me from his team. I
was livid at the injustice and the perceived politics
involved in his decision. I was also deeply hurt and
embarrassed. "I'll show him," I thought. "I'll just
boycott the games. I won't go as a fan, because I no
longer am one. I'll bad-mouth him and the other
players he chose ahead of me. I won't talk to him,
acknowledge him, or say anything positive about
him for the rest of my life. This is not fair!"

As you might imagine, the coach wasn't fixated
on cutting loose yet another mediocre ballplayer.
He'd cut hundreds through the years. He also wasn't

losing sleep over my decision to cut him off from the pleasure of my company. But I was. Resentment and bitterness were absolutely eating me up. I had to forgive him—not for his sake, but for mine. I didn't even tell him I had to forgive him. He hadn't given it a second thought. I just knew that the freedom of forgiveness had to feel a lot better than this self-imposed prison of pity.

It may have been that light bulb-over-the-head realization that led me to search through the Scriptures in an effort to do a little cost-benefit analysis on bitterness. I gotta tell you, the results were pretty ugly. What I found is that there is a tremendous cost—and absolutely zero benefit— associated with bitterness in our lives. Left to grow and fester, it truly can become one of those weapons of mass destruction.

Let me give you just a brief sampling of the ways that destruction can take place. And I'll include the Scripture references where you can go to get the full picture of how bitterness can:

- *Blind us spiritually.* If we continue to hate other people, if we hold a grudge against them, then we just spend our lives stumbling around in darkness. Bitterness sucks the life right out of our souls (1 John 2:9–11).

- *Impede our prayers.* I've discovered that when I am bitter toward another person, it affects my prayers. It's as if God is saying, "Listen, Mike. You need to go to him or her before we really talk about this. You've got a horizontal relationship you need to get right before our vertical one can be right" (Mark 11:25 and 1 Peter 3:7).

- *Undermine our relationships.* In short, bitterness leaks. It's insidious by nature, and it oozes into all kinds of relationships, even affecting innocent bystanders like our kids. God says you've got to dig up bitterness by the root, because otherwise it will spread and infect all your relationships (Heb. 12:15).

- *Steal our freedom.* Jesus said that bitterness can become our own prison. We say, "That person hurt me; they need to pay!" But if we hang onto our anger and resist forgiveness, guess who *really* pays. Guess who can get locked up with a life sentence (Matt. 18:21–35)!

- *Cheapen our worship.* When I go to church with the desire to worship God by offering my gifts, but arrive there with a heart full of bitterness, God reminds me to hang on a second. "You go make it right with that person first. Then you come back and we can have an authentic worship experience."

The truth is, you can't sing, "I love you, Lord," if you still hate a person (Matt. 5:23–24; 1 John 4:20).

- *Downgrade our humanity.* King David said bitterness completely changed his whole personality, his whole attitude—and not in a positive way. "I became like an ignorant brut beast," he wrote, admitting that he was so consumed by bitterness that his humanity was severely downgraded to animalistic instincts (Ps. 73:21–22, paraphrase).

- *Skew our discernment.* When we're bitter, we get very self-centered and, instead of depending on God for direction, we just take matters into our own angry hands. And what about the decisions we make in the midst of all these negative emotions? They can be disastrous (Prov. 28:14).

- *Destroy our health.* I love it when modern science verifies what was stated in the Bible thousands of years earlier. I'm sure you're aware that medical science shows, in study after study, that bitterness can ruin our health. It not only wreaks havoc in our relationships, it tears up our bodies—leaking into our joints and seeping into our stomachs. Have you ever ranted that someone "is a real pain in the neck"? Well, you know what? You're probably right! And that pain in your neck or your back (or somewhere even farther south) may well be pain you invite that person to inflict on you — simply by holding onto all that bitterness toward them. Look at what Job 21:23–25 (GN) has to say: "Some people stay healthy till the day they die; they die happy and at ease, their bodies well-nourished. Others have no happiness at all; they live and die with bitter hearts." Wow. How would you like that one inscribed on your tombstone? "Here lies _____, who lived and died with a bitter heart."

Not so much, I'd guess. And the good news is that there's an effective antidote to this bitter poison. There is a great alternative to spending your days locked up in a prison of anger and resentment because you can't forgive someone who was unable to give you an unfailing love. The keys are in your prison cell. You can *choose to forgive* that person; the price of anything else is way too high.

> What I found is that there
> is a tremendous cost —
> and absolutely zero benefit —
> associated with bitterness
> in our lives.

Forgiveness is letting go of the pain and the past and the resentment. You forgive in order to heal. You look at what God has done in response to your own sin and then ask for the strength to forgive in the same way. You give up your right to get even, and you trust the justice of God as you lean into his grace and mercy.

You need to know that forgiving is not forgetting. People say "forgive and forget," but I'm not sure that's possible — or even healthy. Wounds leave scars. Forgiveness does not mean you have to pretend something never happened. It is not saying, "No big deal." It *did* happen. It *was* a big deal. So it's not about forgetting what has happened; it's about giving up your right to get even for it. And in doing that, you align yourself with God's way of stopping the cycle of abuse, which enables you to start walking freely.

I'm not saying it's easy. You may say, "But they hurt me bad." Yes, and if you hang onto un-forgiveness, they will continue to hurt you. I've known people who were hurt twenty or thirty years ago, and they just keep getting hurt and hurt and hurt, because they keep reliving their pain; they keep hanging onto the bitterness toward the person who wronged them. Forgiveness, on the other hand, allows God to deeply touch your emotional core and enables you to release both the pain and the one who caused it. When you embrace the forgiveness God has lavished on you, it helps you to really forgive from your heart. Healing takes time. But the goal of forgiveness is freedom, and in a single moment, you can make that *choice* to live freely.

FORGIVENESS IS A CHOICE

My mother-in-law, Molly Watts, is one great lady. You know how people make mother-in-law jokes and such? Well, I don't. This woman is flat-out cool. She's fun, caring, creative, and real. She loves God, and she gave birth to one hot daughter! She's a gardening maniac, a member of the Red Hat Society, and a poet.

A lot of Molly's poetry flows out of her life experiences—when something wonderful happens, she writes about it; when something awful happens, she does the same. Not long ago, she wrote a poem called "Forgiveness," an earthy but honest prayer she prayed after an encounter with a perpetually nasty neighbor.

> *Dear Lord, it's me again.*
> *Have you got a little time?*
> *It will only take a minute;*
> *I have something on my mind.*

IDENTITY THEFT

You know I've got this neighbor
and your help I'll have to seek,
for I find it very difficult
to turn the other cheek.
You see, we've got two poodles
that we've come to love a lot,
and, Lord, you know that dogs
must go outside to use the pot.
Most always they stay in our yard;
they don't stray far from home.
But last Thursday they decided
to her front yard they would roam.
Lord, they don't know any better,
and they didn't mean no harm,
but they made a small deposit
in the middle of her lawn.
Well, she went and got her shovel
and with words a little scorched,
she marched up to my door
and, Lord, she threw it on my porch!
"Love thy neighbor as thyself"
are words that came from you,
and if I want to get to heaven,
I must want that for her too.
So I am trying to love her,
even though it's sometimes hard,
and I'm making sure my poodles
do not wander to her yard.

I pray she'll get to heaven,
  but should there be no one around,
could you grant me just one wish
  and put some dog-do in her crown?

This is a true story! Just a real prayer that came from an honest place. You might be wondering, "And exactly how does this represent forgiveness?" Well, Molly began to wonder that, too. So after her cathartic piece of prose, she thought a little while and added a few more lines to represent God's response to her prayer.

My child, I heard you praying,
  and I've listened to your plea.
I think I have an answer
  if you'll listen now to me.
When both you and your neighbor
  have been up here for awhile,
Perhaps she'll dance the golden streets
  and step in a great big pile.
Then, my child, you'll go to her
  and help her to her seat,
and with your towel and basin,
  you will humbly wash her feet.

Molly understands forgiveness. She knows it's a *choice*—one that each of us can make. In fact, the Bible tells us it's a choice we *must* make. The apostle Paul tells us we really have no other viable option: "Make allowance for each other's faults [no matter how nasty, mean, or hard-hearted the other person is] and forgive the person who offends you. Remember, the Lord forgave you, so you *must* forgive others" (Col. 3:13, emphasis added).

I've discovered that it's only by the grace of God that we can pull off something like that. I love what author Brennan Manning says: "If we want to truly love, we must return again and again to the great love of the Great Lover." It is only when you allow God to love you and to experience his unfailing love—his unconditional grace and mercy—that you'll be able to extend the same kind of grace and mercy to another person, especially the person who has hurt you.

THE GREAT LOVER

Remember what Solomon said? "What a person desires is *unfailing love.*" I looked through the Bible and found that the little phrase "unfailing love" is used more than forty times—and every time, it is used in connection with the only one who can actually give unfailing love to us. Let's look at just a few uses of the phrase in the book of Psalms:

- "*Unfailing love* surrounds those who trust the LORD" (Ps. 32:10).

- "The LORD loves righteousness and justice; the earth is full of his *unfailing love*" (Ps. 33:5 NIV).

- "Hope in the LORD; for with the LORD there is *unfailing love* and an overflowing supply of salvation" (Ps. 130:7, emphasis added).

- "Show me your *unfailing love* in wonderful ways. You save with your strength those who seek refuge from their enemies. Guard me as the apple of your eye. Hide me in the shadow of your wings" (Ps. 17:7–8, emphasis added). Did you know that— that you are the apple of God's eye?

We all long to be loved with a love like that, don't we? We all long to be the apple of someone's eye. We all yearn to hear someone say, "I love you." We're all looking for an unfailing love—a love that is constant, a love that will not disappoint, one that is compassionate, dependable, and unconditional. A love that is perfect. You see, deep within our hearts is a God-shaped hole. A perfect fit for Jesus in every way. No heart is too big; no heart is too small. Jesus is the answer. He fits them all.

Perhaps you may be thinking, "Yeah, yeah, yeah, I hear you talking about this Jesus thing and all that, but I need somebody. I need somebody in my life. You don't know how lonely I've been since my husband walked out on me." If you are lonely and feeling that something has been ripped from your life, listen to what the Great Lover says to you: "Do not be afraid; you will not be put to shame. Do not fear disgrace; you will not be humiliated ... for your Maker is your husband—the LORD Almighty is his name" (Isa. 54:4–5 TNIV).

It is only when you allow God
to love you and to experience
his unfailing love—
his unconditional grace and mercy—
that you'll be able to extend
the same kind of grace and mercy to
another person,
especially the person
who has hurt you.

"Yes, but you're not in a family like mine," you might say. "My parents don't give a rip about me. I've never heard them say, 'I love you.' In fact, they've even told me they wish I'd never been born." Or maybe you're living with constant tension because some pretty intense family splintering is going on. Then again, your loneliness may not be about conflict at all—maybe you live alone in an unfamiliar city or on a college campus where any sense of family feels really distant. Maybe you've been separated from your family for a long, long time. Or your children have left, and your nest feels terribly empty. Well, look at what the Bible says to you: "A father to the fatherless, a defender of widows, is God in his holy dwelling. *God sets the lonely in families*" (Ps. 68:5–6 NIV, emphasis added). I just love that last line, don't you? *God sets the lonely in families.*

I recently received an email addressed "To the Family" at our church. It was written by a young woman who, six years earlier, had lost her identity after the collapse of a relationship she'd counted on to provide her with unfailing love. The letter tells her story:

> I am twenty-nine years old, and I am writing to say thank you. About six years ago I began a relationship with a man I truly believed I would marry. After five years together, some good and some bad, the relationship ended abruptly. My whole life changed in an instant, and I never saw

it coming. In one moment, I went from being happy, or so I thought, to feeling like my whole life had been taken away from me. I was devastated. During my relationship with this man, I lost my whole sense of self—I somehow ended up living my life not for me, but for him. When he left, I felt deserted, like I'd been left in this lonely dark place with no light. I was lost.

She went on to explain how she used sleeping pills to alleviate her pain. "I didn't know how to get through the day," she wrote. "I no longer felt like a complete person." So every day she self-medicated the minute she got home from work. "This was my life—if you could call it that," she explained. "Day in and day out, all I had to look forward to was going to work, coming home to sleep, and then going back to work again."

Then one weekend, she ended up at our church. She didn't explain how or why that happened, but she went into great detail about what she experienced that morning—the atmosphere, the people, the music, and the message. She didn't know how this could be, but she felt like everything she heard from the platform was spoken directly to her.

"I sat there and listened to every word," she wrote. "By the middle of the service I felt something in me come alive—something I hadn't felt in years. I finally was regaining peace."

She felt so different, in fact, that she decided to take a pass on the sleeping pills when she got home that day; in fact, she wrote in her letter that she hadn't taken another pill in the six months since attending that first church service. "I am no longer afraid. I have a family!" she continued. "I wake up every morning with a smile, and my attitude toward everyday life has done a total 180. I now look at life as a gift, something that was given to me for a purpose."

I had a chance to talk with this woman a few weeks after her letter arrived. We met in the church lobby after a service, and she came with four new friends who had all been baptized together just a few days earlier. "Families," I thought. "The Lord sets the lonely in families."

He wants to do that for you, too. God made you for community. He longs to bring you to a place where you don't feel alone or unloved. Maybe even right now you sense him telling you to take a risk and be known. Step out of the shadows, drop the anonymity, start walking toward a place of authentic community. He's got family waiting for you.

WITHIN OUR GRASP

God's unfailing love has always been available for such transformation. The apostle Paul addressed that availability as he prayed one of the most fervent prayers in the whole Bible, for a church in the city of Ephesus. This is a great prayer, one you might even want to commit to memory:

> *I pray that from his glorious, unlimited resources he will give you mighty inner strength through his Holy Spirit. And I pray that Christ will be more and more at home in your hearts as you trust in him. May your roots go down deep into the soil of God's marvelous love. And may you have the power to understand, as all God's people should, how wide, how long, how high, and how deep his love really is. May you experience the love of Christ, though it is so great you will never fully understand it. Then you will be filled with the fullness of life and power that comes from God. (Ephesians 3:16–19)*

Let's look a little closer at one of the phrases in that Scripture, the one that says "And may you have the power to *understand*, as all God's people should ..." I did a little word study on the ancient Greek word for "understand," which might better be understood as "grasp." As the word is used here,

46

it actually means to "rust," or to "eat all the way through." So do you see what Paul is saying here? "My prayer is that you would let the high, wide, deep, long love of God *eat all the way through* you. That you would truly *grasp* what it means to be loved with an unfailing love; that you would be completely captured by that."

We don't always go that deep, you know?

I don't know whether that Tupperware ball should get any of the credit, but our youngest son Drew has turned out to be a really, really smart guy. I mean the kid's got a photographic memory. Before a test he'll get out his notes, look at them a few times, and then completely ace the exam. But ask him later if he has a *grasp* of chemistry or trigonometry. Ask him if he truly *grasps* Ancient World Civ. 401. Sure, he received A's in those classes, but he didn't really want to let that knowledge "eat all the way through" him; he just wanted to ace the tests.

I know lots of people who do that with the Bible. They scan through it, hoping to "pass the test." They might memorize the Lord's Prayer and the Ten Commandments—maybe even the "For God so loved the world" verse in John 3. But they never really *grasp* how high and how deep and how long and how wide God's love for them actually is.

And you know, that skim-the-surface acquaintance with God's Word plays itself out in relationships, too. Because even though many of those individuals have been going to church for years and could kill you in a game of Bible trivia, they can be among the most mean-spirited, judgmental, critical, cynical, ornery kinds of people you've ever known. Their relationships are lousy. They hurt their families. They misuse their friendships. They paint on a smile, show up for church, and do the religion thing, singing a few songs, giving a few bucks, and listening to a few sermons. But they never really *grasp* the love God has for them. They never really get to know God, so they never really get to know themselves. And their identity gets all screwed up as they go through life looking for acceptance, security, and significance — and then wrecking relationships that aren't able to give them those things.

BOURNE AGAIN?

Did you see the movie where Matt Damon's character is found floating facedown in the sea? Some fishermen pull him out of the water and onto their boat. They treat his gunshot wound, revive him, and care for him. Then they drop him off at a dock in a city he's never seen — or at least one he doesn't remember ever seeing. He doesn't know who he is. He doesn't know who anybody else is. But he puts together the few clues he has, and eventually those clues lead him to a bank. He fakes his way in and discovers that they remember him there, which somehow enables him to get into his safe deposit box. Inside, he finds a stack of money, a gun, and about a dozen passports—each with his picture on it, but all with different names. Do you remember the name of this movie? It was *The Bourne Identity*, and it was all about a guy trying to figure out who he is.

Back in the days when *I* was facedown and floating, I was trying to figure out who I was, as well. I wouldn't say I was from a dysfunctional family, but it wasn't super functional either. My dad was a great guy, but he was also bipolar and a compulsive gambler. My mom, probably because of broken trust and the fear of losing everything, was pretty controlling. A lot of yelling, arguing, and uncertainty swirled around our home. I was embarrassed to bring friends there because I just never knew what was going to happen.

I was also smaller than most of my peers, which led to a degree of insecurity. And I was an only child, so I felt alone quite a bit. I went to church but didn't have a clue about the love of God. So I faked my spirituality and became a pretty slick chameleon. Alright, enough. This is starting to sound like a counseling session. Suffice it to say that I became an extremely insecure approval addict, who lived like hell but hoped he would go to heaven.

Insecurity is a pretty miserable existence and plays itself out in some very destructive ways. And being phony? Whew! That's really exhausting. One life is hard enough, never mind trying to live two! So as a tired, confused, and eventually broken seventeen-year-old guy, I began seeking after an authentic relationship with the God I knew was there. Yeah, I'd always known he was there, but I never really knew him or how he felt about me.

I started reading through the Bible. And I found that I, too, have a Bourne—uh, make that a born-again—identity. It revolutionized my life to learn that through Jesus Christ, we can all discover who we really are.

One of Jesus's best friends was a guy named John, who pretty much identified himself as "just a guy who Jesus loves" (John 21:20). John wrote, "See what great love the Father has lavished on us, that we should be called children of God! And that is what we are!" (1 John 3:1 TNIV). He also wrote, "Yet to all who did receive him [Jesus], to those who believed in his name, he gave the right to become children of God" (John 1:12 TNIV).

Do you see the little mathematical equation underlying what he says? It's really very simple:

Believe + Receive = Become

The Bible says the first step toward reclaiming our identity is to *believe* that Jesus Christ is the Son of God. Believe that he is the way, the truth, and the life as he said he is. Believe that he was born, that he lived, and that he died. Believe that he rose from the grave and that he's coming back again. And believe that Jesus Christ is the substitution for the penalty of your sin, that he took on your punishment for all the wrong things you've ever done.

Believing is much more than just giving mental assent to something. Believing *in* God and actually *believing* God are two different things. Maybe you've believed in God for a long time, but you've never let the truth that God took your place on a cross eat all the way through you. When you believe God, you trust that what he says about himself—and what he says about you—is absolutely true. You renew your mind to the truth that it's his grace that sets you free. The truth of his unfailing love becomes the foundation for your life. You believe—*really* believe.

Now add in the *receive* part of that equation. A gift is something you receive, and the grace of God through Jesus Christ is a gift. "For God so loved the world, that he *gave* his only Son." To receive a gift like this requires humility. You say, "Jesus Christ, I acknowledge the truth about my sin and I want to receive the free offer of your grace in my life. I receive your offer of an unfailing love that washes away my sin and forgives me for all my screwups and moral failures. I want that grace applied to my life."

Wherever you are on your spiritual journey, the equation is the same: Believe + Receive = Become. "... to all who did receive him, to those who believed in his name, he gave the right to become the children of God." That is who you are!

> When you believe God,
> you trust that what
> he says about himself —
> and what he says about you —
> is absolutely true.

If we children would listen to our Father and begin to really grasp his love for us, then our insecurity levels would go way down. Our confidence in Christ would go way up. Our hunger for approval and acceptance would be satisfied. And our behavior would begin to reflect what our minds now know to be true. Define yourself as a person who is radically loved by God. This is your true self. Any other identity is an illusion.

God loves you lavishly. And when you trust in his Word, rest in his love, and really believe him, he becomes the friend who never leaves you or forsakes you. He becomes the one who is always trustworthy. His Holy Spirit will "enlighten the eyes of your heart" (Eph. 1:18 TNIV) and give you the discernment to recognize any deception that keeps you locked up in unhealthy relationships.

In his book *Abba's Child*, Brennan Manning explains how this works: "When we freely assent to the mystery of our belovedness and accept our core identity as Abba's child, we slowly gain autonomy from controlling relationships. We become inner-directed rather than outer-determined. The fleeting flashes of pleasure or pain caused by the affirmation or deprivation of others will never entirely disappear, but their power to induce self-betrayal will be diminished."

I have learned that when we grow closer to Jesus and we feel more and more grateful for his sacrifice and constant friendship, we become very jealous for him. Any relationship that threatens or pulls me away from my relationship with Christ is a sign of the evil one (the original identity thief) trying to hack into my heart and mess up my life.

Return to the great love of the Great Lover. *Believe* what he says. Maybe you need to get honest and tell him, "God, I'm still trying to cram a lot of square shapes into the round hole in my life. I get distracted and start looking to stuff and other people to give me what only you can give. I *receive* and accept your invitation to work on me from the inside out. I will renew my mind to your truth and cooperate with the transforming power of your Holy Spirit every day, because I want to *become* the person I was meant to be. I want to really grasp your love and find my true identity as a treasured child of the Most High God. I give you permission to lead my life."

You see, deep within our hearts is a God-shaped hole. A perfect fit for Jesus in every way. No heart is too big, no heart is too small. Jesus is the answer; he fits them all.

Accepted. Secure. Significant. What a person desires is an unfailing love. Isn't that what you're looking for? I know I was—and I found it. So with all due respect to Jerry Maguire, *Jesus Christ* completes me. He is the God of unfailing love who wants to complete you too, in a way that gives you back your true identity.

Accepted. Secure. Significant.
What a person desires
is an unfailing love.
Isn't that what you're looking for?

2

MUGGED
BY THE MIRROR

've heard them all: "chrome-dome," "solar panel for a love machine," "God only made a few perfect heads; the rest he covered with hair," ad nauseum, etc., ibid—on and on they go. So I just smiled politely when they gave me their gift. My friends thought it was hilarious to present me with a smooth piece of bristle-free wood inscribed with the words, "Bald man's hairbrush." Funny. That wild and wacky Cracker Barrel gift shop.

But I kept it. I set it on my shelf right below the Tupperware ball, right next to the office window. Whenever I glance that way, it's a reminder not to take my follicly challenged self too seriously. In fact, I see it as one less thing to worry about.

Can you imagine me standing in front of a mirror actually trying to use that hairbrush? It would be as futile as uttering to myself that famous line from former New York Jets quarterback Joe Namath, who reportedly said to his reflection each morning, "I can't wait until tomorrow, 'cause I get better looking every day!"

What do *you* say when you stand in front of the mirror? What do you see? What do you think and feel? Any chance you might be wondering, "What do *they* see?" or "What will they *think*?" or "Will they *like* what they see?"

Don't get me wrong, I think we all want to look good. I mean, there's a little piece of healthy vanity (is that an oxymoron?) in all of us that makes us want to look our best, that wants to be noticed and considered attractive. Sometimes I think I really don't care about the way I look. But then I stand up to teach at my church — from a stage flanked by two giant IMAG screens that make the tiny zit on my forehead look about the size of a trash can lid. And you know what? I do care after all!

Not only do we all care, but we all tend to wrestle with insecurities about our appearance. Guys, have you ever worked out at your gym, standing in front of a mirror as you curled your seventy-, your eighty-, okay your *twenty*-pound dumbbells? As you watch your muscles strain and flex, you begin to think, "Dude! I am ripped!" And that feels pretty great until this other guy walks up next to you — this *huge* other guy, with his two-hundred-pound bar. He's standing there pumping and puffing, and you notice his biceps are about twice the size of your thighs. That's when you look at yourself and say, "Oh, man, I'm not ripped. I'm ripped *off*!"

In mere seconds, all that adrenaline, all that joy, all that confidence you had in yourself was just sucked away—eliminated by the insecurities and inadequacies that rushed in to take their place. What happened here? You just got mugged by the mirror.

That happens a lot these days because, by all accounts, we live in a culture obsessed with physical beauty. Take the TV shows that feed on our preoccupation. There's *Extreme Makeover*, of course, and MTV's *I Want a Famous Face*. You may have watched *Dr. 90210*, and you've probably at least heard about *The Swan*. That's where they put a number of (as they call them) "ugly ducklings" through all kinds of cosmetic surgeries in an effort to turn them into "beautiful swans." Then at the end of the season, they hold a beauty pageant in which the winner is crowned "the fairest of them all." What happens, I wonder, to all those women except one, who in the end find they're still not quite beautiful enough to claim the identity they crave?

And don't be tempted to think this is solely a women's issue. Not long ago, MTV followed around a young man named Luke. Here was a guy obsessed with working out—and he was in phenomenal shape. But as he stood in front of the workout mirror, he kept noticing that his calves weren't quite keeping up with the rest of his body. So Luke decided to have calf implants. And no, I am not kidding.

Luke's surgery was more complex than planned, and his rehab took longer than usual. But finally he was through it and ready to go. He couldn't wait to go clubbing and show off his new pumped-up lower legs. He was so excited!

The cameras followed him into the clubs, recording his efforts to pick up girls. But the girls weren't interested—in fact, they all thought his calf implants were just flat-out weird. They laughed at him and left him to dance alone by the bar—and while lots of viewers undoubtedly considered all of this very entertaining, it actually was incredibly sad. Because it clearly demonstrates how our obsession with the way we look and the image we project can steal away our very identity.

WHAT'S NORMAL?

Michelle Graham has written an insightful, funny, honest, helpful book for women, entitled *Wanting to Be Her.* In the book, she talks about how, in 1959, a new kid arrived on the block and became the cultural icon of what the ideal woman needed to look like. Any clue who that might be? You're exactly right—her name was Barbie.

You know what? Barbie's proportions make her an anatomical freak! In order for her legs to be that long, she'd need to be well over seven feet tall. She'd have to be missing about four ribs and most of her internal organs to achieve that figure. Nevertheless, she was soon deemed the "perfect" woman—the model that real women (complete with bones, hearts, lungs, and other necessities) considered the ideal.

For some Barbie owners, this idealization became personal—and an objective they would spend a lifetime trying to achieve. "This is the image that has been marketed to young girls all over the world as an inspiration to womanhood, and we eat it up," Graham writes. "Barbie has become a $1.5 billion a year industry. Now don't worry, I'm not on a Barbie burning crusade and I'm certainly no expert on the psychological effects of Barbie on young children. But, I do know, at a very young age, I bought into the idea that unless my Barbie was physically perfect, she wasn't as good as the other Barbies on the block."

For Graham, the pursuit of such perfection continued. "As I grew into adulthood, I left my Barbie behind. Unfortunately, I struggle with the belief that unless I am physically perfect, I somehow am not as valuable as everybody else. Barbie moved out, and Victoria's Secret moved in. Yeah, there's nothing quite like a glance at a Victoria's Secret catalog to invoke a flood of insecurities and feelings of disappointment."

Michelle is hardly alone in her insecurities. In fact, a recent survey reported that 70 percent of women felt depressed, guilty, and shameful after looking at a fashion magazine for only three minutes. Those women have bought into the lie that says our value is directly proportionate to our physical attractiveness.

Of course, there is big business in perpetuating and accommodating that lie. Beauty-aid companies spend $1.5 billion annually on advertising, and Americans eagerly respond. In fact, we spent more than $20 billion on cosmetics last year—$2 billion of it on hair care products alone. (I'm saving a fortune!) We spent $74 billion on diet foods, a concept that might be pretty difficult to explain to children in some impoverished countries. And 7.4 million of us will undergo cosmetic surgery in the next year. At this point, five out of six of those patients will be women, but men are increasingly joining their ranks.

What does all this mean? It means we're getting mugged by the mirror. We're buying a lie that equates looking a certain way with being happy, contented, and showered with unfailing love.

Here's how the lie plays itself out in our heads ... *If I'm attractive enough to other people, I will be accepted and admired. I will be respected, significant, and loved. I will be worthwhile. I will be enough. And once that happens, all my problems will be resolved; my life will fall into place. Members of the opposite sex will find me irresistible. Employers will want to hire me. Friends will want to be with me. Friends will want to be me!*

> We're buying a lie that equates
> looking a certain way
> with being happy, contented, and
> showered with unfailing love.

Although we're surrounded by a culture that reinforces these lies every single day, every now and then there's an effort to buck that trend. Did you see the Dove soap ads that featured non-supermodels posing in plain white underwear, smiling from various magazine pages and billboards?

These women, who ranged from size eight to sixteen, were part of a marketing campaign generated by the results of a fascinating global survey on beauty—one that indicated 89 percent of the world's women wished beauty could be redefined.

Survey participants said they hoped our culture would lose its obsession with the tall, ultra-thin image of perfection (think Barbie). They dared to imagine a world in which women would learn to, in their words, "be comfortable in our own skin."

The women of different weights, heights, builds, and colors who appeared in this advertising campaign might have been on the leading edge of such a transition, but here in the United States, the response was mostly negative. Reportedly, the most frequent response to these ads was, "We don't want to look at a bunch of out-of-shape women."

Apparently, we prefer to look at women who are just this side of starvation. If that seems like an overstatement, consider the fact that for the past three decades, the majority of Miss America winners have had body mass indexes that lie within the range of malnutrition. And that while the average American woman is five foot three and weighs 152 pounds, the average model is five foot nine and weighs just 109.

Even then, the image is not always what it seems. You do know, don't you, that professionals are paid big bucks to perpetuate the flawless look celebrities crave? That can mean out-of-sight duct tape pulling or lifting in strategic locations. It can mean hours in makeup application—and I'm not just talking lipstick and mascara here. Makeup artists can even make a guy look like he's got six-pack abs, instead of the two-liter variety I carry around!

And it's amazing how photos can be digitally altered. Did you see the whittled down promotional shot of Katie Couric as she prepared to begin anchoring the "CBS Evening News"? *Newsweek* ran the original photo side by side with the touched-up version in which Katie seemed to have dropped twenty pounds. The accompanying article reported, "A CBS spokesman said an 'overzealous' employee had digitally altered the photo to make her appear slimmer, without Couric's or CBS's approval." As for Katie, she preferred the original photo, she said, "because there is more of me to love."*

The bottom line is that most of us can't come close to achieving these unrealistic images—genetically, our bodies just can't pull it off.

---

*Jac Chebatovis, "The Hot Skinny on Katie's New Look," *Newsweek*, September 11, 2006, 63.

Moreover, it can be very unhealthy to even try. And as the lie is perpetuated and reinforced, way too many people—especially young girls—are literally dying in their efforts to achieve an unattainable image.

I don't know about you, but to me the whole thing sounds incredibly *sinister.* (A strong word, I know, but I am not exaggerating.) And you know why? Because it's all based on a lie that comes straight out of the depths of hell. It's a plan that the enemy of our souls has had from the beginning to distort our image, to distort the image of God, and to steal our identity.

Jesus called that enemy the Father of Lies and a thief that "comes only to steal and kill and destroy" (John 10:10 NIV). In fact the whole image thing started a very long time ago, when that identity thief entered a garden called Eden. Take a look:

> Then God said, "Let us make people in our image, to be like ourselves. They will be masters over all life— the fish in the sea, the birds in the sky, and all the livestock, wild animals, and small animals. So God created people in his own image; God patterned them after himself; male and female he created them.... Then God looked over all he had made, and he saw that it was excellent in every way. (Genesis 1:26–27, 31, emphasis added)

Read a little further and you pick up a sense of the healthy self-image those first human beings initially enjoyed: "Now the man and his wife were both naked, but they felt no shame" (Gen. 2:25). They were walking with God and with each other. They were made in God's image. And they seemed perfectly comfortable with the "excellent" bodies they were given.

But the story begins to shift in chapter 3. Enter the thief, disguised here as a serpent: Now the serpent was the shrewdest of all the creatures the LORD God had made. "Really?" he asked the woman. "Did God really say you must not eat any of the fruit in the garden?" (Gen. 3:1).

Man, the thief has been using that line since the beginning of time! Hasn't he come to you and said, "Did God really say that? Come on. Did God really say he loves you? Are you sure? Did God really say that you're accepted, secure, and significant? Did he really? Did God say you're beautiful? Did he say you're enough? Did God really say you're the apple of his eye? Did God really say ...?" But let's get back to the story.

Eve begins her response with a clarification. "'Of course we may eat it,' the woman told him. 'It's only the fruit from the tree at the center of the garden that we are not allowed to eat'" (Gen. 3:2–3). The serpent then basically tells Eve that God is on a big ego trip; in fact, God's holding out on her. " 'You won't die!' the serpent hissed. 'God knows that your eyes will be opened when you eat it. You will become just like God, knowing everything, both good and evil' " (Gen. 3:4–5).

So they stand in the garden, that man and that woman, and they buy the lie. They figure, "You know what? That serpent's right. God *is* holding back on us." Feeling "less than" now, they look at their reflections and decide they are no longer satisfied to be made in the image of their Creator. "You lied to us, God!" They pick the fruit from the forbidden tree and immediately they feel deep shame—they embraced a distorted image rather than their God-given image. And as they search for a way to cover up, the thief slithers away, deeply satisfied.

PASSING ALONG THE LIE

Ever since that day, we've been trying to cover up our shame, too. We go through life looking at a distorted image, unsatisfied with being created in the image of God and striving to create another image for ourselves. Trouble is, this substitute image pulls us further and further away from God and the truth—and ironically, further and further away

from the unfailing love and deep satisfaction we so
desperately desire.

We go through life
looking at a distorted image,
unsatisfied with being created
in the image of God
and striving to create
another image for ourselves.

But as perverse and backward as it all is, we just
keep buying the lie. In fact, we don't just buy it
for ourselves, but we pass it along like a really bad
strain of the flu. The movie *Spanglish* includes a
scene in which an extremely insecure mom returns
from a shopping spree with new clothes for her
teenage daughter Bernie, a wonderful, funny, bright,
fourteen-year-old with curly hair and braces on her
teeth. Bernie is studying for a history test with her
dad when the mom bursts into the room with the
new clothes. And Bernie is excited—until she finds
that everything her mom bought for her is several
sizes too small. Her self-image is deeply wounded
as her mom says, "You're gonna do it, Bernie.
You're gonna lose that weight and you're gonna look
beautiful."

When I saw that scene, I sat there stunned and brokenhearted. Yes, it was just a movie. But it was art imitating life, because the actual examples of how we inflict this lie, even on those we love, are everywhere. It will not be easy to read, but let me share an email I received not long ago from a young woman at my church.

She began by telling me she had married in her early twenties—noting that, at the time, she was five feet six inches tall and weighed 115 pounds. A couple years later and a few pounds heavier, she was enduring serious physical abuse from her husband. They divorced, but the trauma of what she had been through triggered an eating disorder. "I started to make myself throw up any time I ate too much or felt like I was gaining weight," she said. By the time she was down to 105 pounds, though, the pain from the vomiting and constant exercising became unbearable. She successfully fought back her desire to purge.

Things improved after that. Eventually she remarried, and at age thirty-two, had a child. She dropped her baby weight and stabilized. All was well for several years, until the medicine she needed for a subsequent medical condition caused her to gain eighteen pounds in less than three months. She changed medications, but it didn't help. She dieted and walked in an effort to lose the weight in a healthy way. But in the six months before writing to me, she had gained five additional pounds.

The day before she wrote, her dad had showed up for one of his very infrequent visits.

> He walked up to me, put his hand across my waist and said, "What happened to my skinny girl? Where did that pretty little girl go? You've gotten so big." I broke into tears. In fact, I just keep crying. At almost forty years of age, I feel so wounded and hurt all over again that I'd love to stick my finger straight down my throat. He said he didn't mean to make me cry and is "sure" I'll be able to "lose the weight."
>
> I hate the way I look—it makes me feel disgusted and deeply sad. I know it isn't supposed to matter, but I can't let go of it. There are so many things so much more important—AIDS, war, poverty. I'm sorry this seems so petty, but I have got to know. Does God care at all about this?

Well, the answer to her (and perhaps your) question, is *yes*. And now let me ask *you* something: What if the words of an insecure mom or an insensitive dad were replaced by loving words of truth from your heavenly Father? Would that make a difference for you?

I hope it will, because I want to offer you four principles and the words from God on which they're based. And since my hope is that these principles will turn the tables on this whole body-image deal, I hope you'll allow me to put them under the heading of ...

SOME VICTORIOUS SECRETS (SORRY!)

Principle One: Know What God Says

It is so important for us to know what God says about us. It is critical that we grasp the truth that we are fearfully and wonderfully made in his image.

You'll recall that earlier in this book we talked about the importance of grasping the wide, long, high, deep love of God. The Scripture noted earlier bears repeating: "May your roots grow down deep into the soil of God's marvelous love. And may you have the power to understand [grasp], as all God's people should, how wide, how long, how high, and how deep his love really is" (Eph. 3:17–18).

We have already learned that the word for "understand" or "grasp" literally means to apprehend, to capture, to rust, to eat all the way through. So the apostle Paul is begging you not to be satisfied with the CliffsNotes version here. He wants you to really, really know how high, how deep, how wide, how long the love of God is for you. To know what his Word says about you. To be captured by his unfailing love. To let it eat you up.

It is so important for us to know
what God says about us.
It is critical that we grasp the truth
that we are fearfully
and wonderfully
made in his image.

Now, when I really grasp what God says about me, I don't have to fret about looking just right in order to be accepted. I already am. I don't have to hide behind the right kind of jeans or shades. I was made with excellence by a God who loves me and who doesn't make mistakes. God tells us that he knit us together with excitement, with hope, with joy, and with precision. The color of our eyes, the color of our skin, the shape of our face, the curl of our hair — none of it is a mistake. And he tells us that through Jesus Christ, we are already accepted, secure, and significant. His love — his *unfailing* love — is "one size fits all."

Drink from the well of what God says in the Bible. Know what he says about himself and about you. Soak in the truth.

I'm into remodeling; Debbie and I sometimes take old houses, fix them up, and flip them for a small profit. In general, I like the demolition part of home improvement a whole lot better than the putting-it-back-together part. Except for wallpapering. Because the worst, absolute worst, part of every project is stripping that paper off the walls. I hate it! I sometimes suspect it might even be the leading cause of divorce in America—and that if you and your spouse can make it through wallpapering, you must have a pretty solid marriage.

The Bible talks about our need to strip away the old and put on the new—kind of like re-wallpapering our minds. "Don't copy the behavior and customs of this world, but let God transform you into a new person by changing the way you think" (Rom. 12:2). When you know what God says and renew your mind daily to the truth, you start to think differently about God, about yourself, about others, and about life. Every day, as you re-wallpaper your mind with the life-changing words of God, your perspective starts to change.

I talk to so many people who wish now that they'd put that discipline into practice years and years ago. And I agree with them that the earlier, the better. That's why Debbie and I encouraged our kids to memorize Colossians 2:8, so they could pray that verse around the breakfast table before they would go off to school each day. "See to it that no one takes you captive through hollow and deceptive philosophy, which depends on human tradition and the basic principles of this world rather than on Christ" (NIV).

You start by renewing your mind to the truth; then, with real determination, you apply it to the challenges of living in this culture. You say, "I refuse to buy the lie any longer. I am not going to let a magazine cover or a bathroom scale take me captive. I will not be held prisoner by the reflection in some silly piece of glass. I will pursue no other image than the image of God in me." You stake your claim on a whole new way of thinking— and on the identity that was yours in the first place.

I've found a practical way to do that. At least it works for me. When I was a kid and had a sick day or one of those rare and coveted snow days, I'd lie on the couch and watch *The Price Is Right*—you know, "Come on down!" Bob Barker (he retired at 137 years old).

Did you ever see the game they call Plinko? Contestants climb to the top of this twelve-foot-tall giant double-sided pegboard and drop a disk through the center of it. This disk works its way through a grid toward the bottom, veering and rolling and eventually landing in a slot labeled $100, $1,000, $10,000, or $0. It really is the "most exciting hour of television!"

Well, there's a verse in Philippians that works like a Plinko grid for me. When I'm thinking negative thoughts, or when some of those accusing whispers come into my head, I kind of drop the thought through this truth grid: "Fix your thoughts on what is true and honorable and right. Think about things that are pure and lovely and admirable. Think about things that are excellent and worthy of praise" (Phil. 4:8).

So when a negative thought pops into your mind and says, "You are so fat," you drop that thought through the grid and say, "Hang on a second . . . no, that's not *true*." Or maybe, "You are so ugly." "Wait . . . that's not *right*." How about, "You'll never turn anyone on with a body like that." "Let me see . . . uh, that's not *pure*." Or maybe, "Oh, I wish I could look like that." "Hold on . . . that's not *admirable*." To my way of thinking, this is what it means to take every thought captive and make it obedient to Christ. If visualizing a Plinko game can help you do that, you're more than welcome to borrow the idea. But you've got to have a truth grid, which God's Word provides.

Once you begin matching up the lies with the truth, you'll see who wins. Knowing the truth — grasping the fact that you are loved with an unfailing love and telling yourself the truth about who you are — affects everything. It has an impact on the way you eat, the way you drink, the way you love, the way you laugh, the way you exercise, the way you play, the way you work, the way you *live*.

My wife is drop-dead gorgeous. Really. She's never graced the cover of a fashion magazine, but in my eyes she is absolutely striking. And do you know when it is that she takes my breath away? Early in the morning when I walk into the family room and see her sitting there in an old flannel robe, hair messed up, no makeup, reading glasses on, Bible open on her lap, highlighter in her hand, soaking in God's Word — working on the inside stuff. And anyone who knows her will tell you, she radiates from the inside out.

Knowing the truth —
grasping the fact that you are loved
with an unfailing love
and telling yourself the truth
about who you are —
affects everything.

79

Know what God says. Grasp it. Memorize it. Let it eat all the way through you. Instead of spending so much time thumbing through the pages of *Seventeen* and *Glamour* and *Muscle & Fitness* and *Sports Illustrated*, looking at those sculpted bodies and thinking, "Wow, if I could only look like that," spend more time turning the pages of Matthew, Mark, Luke, and John, looking at Jesus and going, "Man! If I could only look like *that*!"

Principle Two: See How God Sees

You know, it's one thing to look beautiful; quite another to *be* beautiful. Have you ever met someone who struck you as extremely attractive, only to change your mind once you got to know him or her a little bit? If so, you can relate to the waitress played by Helen Hunt in the movie *As Good As It Gets*, when she says to the grumpy customer played by Jack Nicholson, "You know, when you first came in here, I thought you were handsome. But then you opened your mouth."

You see, beauty or handsomeness is an inside-out kind of thing. At least, that's the way God sees it. Consider what he had to say when he chose a king for the nation of Israel and instructed the prophet Samuel what to look for on the résumé: "But the LORD said to Samuel, 'Do not consider his appearance or his height, for I have rejected him. The LORD does not look at the things human beings look at. People look at the outward appearance, but the LORD looks at the heart'" (1 Sam. 16:7 TNIV).

Actually, nearly all of us have some ability, don't we, to discern whether a person's interior and exterior are in sync? I remember an old TV show about two junk dealers. It was called *Sanford and Son*, and I used to love that show. Fred, Lamont, Grady—all very funny guys. Fred had this sister-in-law, though, whom he couldn't stand. Remember Aunt Esther? She was this nasty, mean, hateful kind of person, and she and Fred were always at odds. Of course, he was pretty mean to her, too, making jokes about how ugly she was and calling her names.

I remember one scene in which Fred walks into the house with a stringer full of fish. Aunt Esther comes into the room at the same moment Lamont asks Fred, "Pop, how did you catch all those fish?" Fred glances over at Esther and says something like, "I was down by the dock, and Esther fell in the lake. All the fish took one look at her ugly face and jumped up on the pier. I just picked them all up."

I never thought I'd be quoting Fred Sanford all these years later, but he had it right when he said, "Beauty is skin deep; ugly goes all the way to the bone." And you know what? Theologically, he's not far off.

The Old Testament includes the story of another Esther, one who was beautiful from the outside in—all the way to the bone. But in the whole book of the Bible dedicated to her story, there's only one mention of her external beauty, which opened a door for God to use her. However, there are ten full chapters about her courage, her intelligence, her leadership, her wisdom, and her compassion—all to explain how this inside-out beautiful woman saved the whole Jewish race from genocide.

Contrast that with another Old Testament account of a physically beautiful person, a guy named Absalom. He was one of King David's sons, and the description of him in 2 Samuel leaves no doubt he could have graced the cover of *People* magazine's annual "Sexiest Man Alive" issue. "Now no one in Israel was as handsome as Absalom. From head to foot, he was the perfect specimen of a man" (2 Sam. 14:25).

On the inside, though, it was a different story. There was nothing beautiful about him. He was prideful. He was arrogant. He was rebellious. He was a violent man who died a violent death. Fred Sanford had him pegged—Absalom's kind of ugly went all the way to the bone.

If we're going to get a handle on this whole beauty-obsession/body-image deal, we're going to have to learn to see how God sees. Take a look at how that's described by the apostle Peter: "Don't be concerned about the outward beauty [or handsomeness] that depends on fancy hairstyles, expensive jewelry, or beautiful clothes. You should be known for the beauty that comes from within, the unfading beauty of a gentle and quiet spirit, which is so precious to God" (1 Peter 3:3–4).

Let me ask you this: Did that Scripture say you shouldn't style your hair? Did it say you are not to wear jewelry? Did it warn that you should not wear hip, cool clothes? No, it did not. It said your beauty should not *depend* on those externals. Instead, your attractiveness should come primarily from the inside. So it's there—on the inside—where we need to focus most of our time and effort.

A lot of us, though, spend a disproportionate amount of energy on the outside stuff. We stand in front of a mirror or our closet for an hour, trying on one outfit after another in an effort to find exactly the right look. We know all the rules about slimming black, no horizontal stripes, exactly how far our pants should sag, or where our pant legs should "break" on our perfectly polished shoes. We spend a lot of time learning *What Not to Wear.*

Allow me to suggest that the Bible has its own hot new trends for this fashion season—except they really aren't new and they're not exactly trends.

Think of them as timeless style. Take this tip, for instance: "So, chosen by God for this new life of love, dress in the wardrobe God picked out for you: compassion, kindness, humility, quiet strength, discipline. Be even-tempered, content with second place, quick to forgive an offense. Forgive as quickly and completely as the Master forgave you. And regardless of what else you put on, wear love. It's your basic, all-purpose garment. Never be without it" (Col. 3:12–14 MSG).

We could really help each other out by occasionally saying something like, "Hey, you know what? That humility looks good on you." Or, "Whoa, you look hot in that compassion!" Or, "You're looking fine in that forgiveness." Or, "Wow, that gentleness fits you so well." We could encourage one another to see how God sees, by highlighting the really beautiful qualities in one another — those character qualities that come from the inside.

Principle Three: Love Who God Loves

Jesus made it clear that life is pretty simple: *Love God. Love people.* He said we should love the Lord our God with all our heart, mind, soul, and strength. And we are to love our neighbors as ourselves.

When we do that — when we love our neighbors enough to serve them — that sure can help to relieve any obsession we have with the way we look. I guess that's because we take our eyes off the mirror when we look out the window.

When you're clipping the toenails of an arthritic eighty-five-year-old woman in a nursing home, you aren't thinking about your split ends or tan lines. When you're working at a soup kitchen for the homeless, you're not counting carbs or fat grams. When you're under the hood of a single mom's car, making repairs to keep it running for her and her three kids, you're not contemplating calf implants!

This kind of refocusing is one of the things I love most about taking groups of people on mission trips. After about three days, everybody looks and smells pretty much the same. You're covered in sweat, mud, concrete, or paint. As you're holding an AIDS orphan or handing a bag of beans and rice to a hungry family, you're just not concerned with your love handles or having the right label in the back of your shirt collar. You are losing yourself in loving others — and reclaiming your true identity in the process.

The prophet Isaiah records God's own words about this: "Is not this the kind of fasting I have chosen: to loose the chains of injustice and untie the cords of the yoke, to set the oppressed free and break every yoke? Is it not to share your food with the hungry and to provide the poor wanderer with shelter—when you see the naked, to clothe him, and not to turn away from your own flesh and blood? *Then your light will break forth like the dawn, and your healing will quickly appear; then your righteousness will go before you, and the glory of the LORD will be your rear guard*" (Isa. 58:6–8 NIV, emphasis added).

Isaiah is saying you can find healing for yourself by not focusing so much *on* yourself! When you love those whom God loves, it puts life into proper perspective. You start to live as a person made in God's image, and all the cultural lies about what your image "ought" to be are revealed for the shallowness they represent.

Let me add just a short but important postscript to this discussion on loving who God loves: if you are going to fully love who God loves, you have to love *yourself*. I'm not talking about selfishness or a look-out-for-number-one kind of attitude. I'm talking about a right estimation of the priceless person God says you are. It's been my experience that when I fail to love the person looking back at me in the mirror, it's also hard to love other people. Ironically, failure to love myself makes me focus way too much on myself.

And way too often, that kind of focus escalates into obsession.

Eating disorder counselor, Monica Dickson, writes:

> I have stared into the eyes of a catatonic young woman who subsisted on half a bagel a day while practicing gymnastics for three hours a day. I have held the dry and withered hand of a twenty-one-year-old who ran ten miles a day on two bowls of Special K with skim milk. I have hugged the shaking bodies of young women who drove endlessly from one gas station to another in the middle of the night buying candy bars, eating them in the car, and throwing them up at the next stop. I've been awakened in the middle of the night by young women terrified by the seizures of vomiting brought on by themselves. I have watched beautiful, bright, young women die.
>
> I have way too many young friends who are right there, right now. It breaks my heart. I say to them — and I want to say to you, if it applies — that if you're struggling with some kind of eating disorder, there is hope. Get help. Don't deny that you've got a problem going on. Get honest with yourself, with God, and with someone you trust. There are treatment centers. There are hospitals. There are great counselors. There are friends, parents, grandparents, and others who want to help.

Get into a community where the talk is healthy, and not so focused on all the externals. I have a good friend who decided to quit her cheerleading squad because all the talk in that environment centered on how to stay below 100 pounds. It wasn't okay to be 101 or 102, she said. You had to be below 100—no matter what weight was actually appropriate for your body. She realized this situation was taking her down a very unhealthy path, so when confronting the coach's expectations didn't help, she walked away.

> It's been my experience
> that when I fail to love the person
> looking back at me in the mirror,
> it's also hard to love other people.

It is possible that you'll need to muster the courage to do something similar. To walk away from unhealthy expectations and relationships and get to a place where you can heal and grow and reclaim your true identity. Find someone who is willing to help you grasp God's love for you—maybe someone else who is working to grasp it, too. Feed yourself on the truth cited in the previous pages—there really *is* healing in his Word.

There is, in fact, Scripture that you might find helpful. Look at this: "They cried to the LORD in their trouble, and he saved them from their distress. He sent out *his word* and healed them; he rescued them from the grave. Let them give thanks to the LORD for his unfailing love and his wonderful deeds for humankind" (Ps. 107:19–21 TNIV, emphasis added).

There is hope and healing in the words of God.

A twenty-year-old girl recently sent me this poem she wrote, titled, "In the Arms of My Father":

> *I sat on the couch*
> *Coffee, music, Bible, sadness.*
> *Feeling unworthy, unloved, discouraged*
> *Broken pieces of myself all around me.*
> *Unwilling to love, unwilling to believe*
> *Waiting, waiting, wanting, needing, feeling....*
> *The arms of my Father around me,*
>   *blanketing me, loving me, assuring me,*
>   *comforting me, accepting me.*
> *"You are worthy, daughter. You are loved.*
>   *You are my most beloved daughter.*
>   *Believe, believe."*
> *As I leaned into his arms, I heard him*
>   *speak those words.*
> *And in that moment I loved myself,*
>   *and believed.*

Whatever you struggle with right now, the key to wholeness is to humble yourself and believe. Believe that what God says about you is absolutely true, and learn to love yourself as he loves you. Then you will be free—with heart, mind, body, and soul—to love who God loves.

Principle Four: Reflect Who God Is

Know what God says. See what God sees. Love who God loves. So you can reflect who God is.

Did you know that when we come into a relationship with God through his Son Jesus Christ, he moves in? Yeah, that's right. Once that happens, God is no longer 'out there somewhere'; he is *in* us! The apostle Paul reminds us: "Don't you know that your body is the temple of the Holy Spirit, who lives in you and was given to you by God? You do not belong to yourself, for God bought you with a high price. So you must honor God with your body" (1 Cor. 6:19–20).

Once you know that the body you live in actually serves as a "temple of the Holy Spirit," it kind of makes you want to take care of the place, doesn't it? Makes you want to step up and declare, "I'm not going to trash the temple anymore. God, you gave me this body and you live in it—so I'm going to treat it well. I'm going to exercise it, feed it the right kind of fuel, and give it the rest it needs. Not so I can bring glory or attention to myself, but so I can honor the One who lives inside."

Just in case you're wondering—yes, it's okay to decorate the temple! It's fine to do a little remodeling, or to make some home improvements as you need to. As long as the goal is to draw attention to the One who resides within. Because when we dress or carry ourselves in a way that invites others to worship our bodies, we rob God of the worship that is due to him alone.

Recently, a man came up to me after church and said, "You know the moon just reflects the light of the sun, right?"

I said, "Yeah."

"So do you know why the moon goes dark?" he asked.

"No, not really," I said.

"Because the world gets in the way," he answered.

Pretty insightful, wouldn't you say?

That conversation made me think of this word from God: "We can be mirrors that brightly reflect the glory of the Lord. And as the Spirit of the Lord works within us, we become more and more like him and reflect his glory even more" (2 Cor. 3:18). Isn't that cool? When we stop getting mugged by the mirror and start to become more and more like

God, he says, "I want to use *you* as the mirror now, to reflect my glory to a watching world."

I had a wonderful thing happen the other day on the basketball court—my mind finally agreed with my body! In the past, my mind would say, "You *can* make that move," but my body would scream back, "What are you *thinking?*" This time, though, I was standing there with the ball in my hands, thinking how I might take my slower defender to the hoop. "I'll fake left, drive hard right, then spin back with a left-handed teardrop shot," said my mind. Then my body piped up, "No way!" And my mind, for once, said, "Yeah, you're right." What a freeing experience—from now on, I'm going to stay outside the three-point line as if it's an electric dog-fence!

When we stop getting mugged
by the mirror and start
to become more and more like God,
he says, "I want to use *you*
as the mirror now, to reflect
my glory to a watching world."

Speaking of aging, which is what that mind-body conversation was really all about, certain Scriptures are becoming more meaningful to me with each passing year. I love the way the Message version of 2 Corinthians 4:16–18 tells it like it is: "So we're not giving up. How could we! Even though on the outside it often looks like things are falling apart on us [Yep!], on the inside, where God is making new life, not a day goes by without his unfolding grace. These hard times are small potatoes compared to the coming good times, the lavish celebration prepared for us. There's far more here than meets the eye. The things we see now are here today, gone tomorrow. But the things we can't see now will last forever."

I occasionally watch the show *Extreme Makeover* because I like, at times, how it takes a person with very low self-esteem—the result, perhaps, of lifelong ridicule over some aspect of their appearance—and gives that person newfound confidence. What a great feeling for the doctors who can give that to them! I mean, the before-and-after pictures are just staggering. When you look at them, you swear they're not of the same person.

I was looking through family photo albums the other day and came across some really old pictures of myself. The "before" and "after" images they reflect are pretty staggering. I'm not kidding—if you saw them, you'd say, "There's no way this is the same guy." For starters, I had a ton of hair—think Michael Landon, *Little House on the Prairie* hair. And

I was really thin—even kind of buff, if you want to know the truth.

Those pictures got me to thinking—about the past, about my own befores and afters, about what people see when they look at another person. And do you know what I concluded I really want? For people to look at me and see the amazing, striking, staggering difference in the "before-and-after-Jesus" pictures of my life.

You see, back before I knew Jesus, I had lots of thick hair, but I was ugly to the bone. I had some pretty tight abs and pecs and all the rest of it, but I made fun of other people who looked less than "normal." Poked fun at their weight, hair, faces, voices, mannerisms, clothes ... as if I were the standard of normalcy. To keep up appearances, I dressed the part. I enjoyed being fashionable, even trendy, and clothes actually hung pretty well on me. But I dressed myself in anger, malice, envy, impure thoughts, lust, and pride. I let the thief distort the image of God in me. I let him steal my identity.

But then I drew close to God and God drew close to me. I started renewing my mind daily with his Word and praying for a change of perspective. I began to replace cultural lies with eternal truth and dropped my thoughts through a different grid. I started finding beauty in the people the world labels ugly, undesirable rejects. And as a result, I began to pour myself into serving their needs instead of always focusing on my external shortcomings. I took really seriously God's desire for me to love him, others, and myself. And you know what? I have a long, long way to go, but through the years—and, may I add, through countless reconstructive "surgeries,"—he's done an extreme makeover on my soul.

The best news is, God's not done yet. And with that internal focus, I just want to say, "I can't wait until tomorrow, 'cause I get better looking every day!"

3

STOLEN
BY SUCCESS

Imagine, if you will, that you are walking with me across the parking lot outside the building where I work. It's a pretty big parking lot in the middle of a pretty big area called Chicagoland. Yeah, the Windy City. We're almost to the building now.

Let's head upstairs to the third floor. You're breathing heavily. I guess we should've taken the elevator, but there's just one more flight. Okay, turn right. We're here. Come on in, and throw your jacket over there in the corner. Welcome to my crib.

Well, it's not my home, it's just my office, so I don't really live here—I'm happy to say I settled that workaholic thing a long time ago. I'm here enough, though, that I want to enjoy the place. And I do. It's not very big and not real organized, but it has a great view and it's functional enough for me.

Just move that stack of papers on the chair over there, and have a seat while I show you around.

My office might not be what you'd expect from a pastor-type; in a word, I guess you could say it's "eclectic"—or at least that's a good description of the collection of odd little things I keep in here. Check out this candy dispenser in the shape of a blue M&M peanut guy shooting a basketball—hit a jumper, get a piece of candy. And here's the car I used to drive. Well, not *that* one, exactly, but a model of the old baby blue '65 Nova I drove in the nineties—a gift my son Derrick made for me when he was ten years old.

I have a mug that proclaims, "Attitude Is Everything," a flag from the fifteenth hole of some obscure golf course, and my collection of hooded sweatshirts and jerseys that I keep over there in the corner. I love my Bubba Gump hat that hangs over the window, as well as my University of Kentucky 1998 National Championship hat signed by my friend, Coach Tubby Smith. And speaking of my home state, here's an empty bottle of Ale-8-One, a Kentucky soft drink that tastes like somebody mixed ginger ale and Mountain Dew, then left it out on the counter until it got really flat. Can't get enough of the stuff.

There's my ashtray from the Las Vegas Hilton (no, I did not steal it), and over here is my set of multicolored juggling balls that were specially designed to relieve stress. (In fact, I am juggling them even as I sit here and type. I am pretty amazing.)

And I wasn't going to point this out, but you're probably wondering about the crystal bowl on the shelf behind me—the one that says "Champion" on it? It's pretty darn impressive. Now, I'm not a great golfer (I tell people I shoot in the seventies, because if it gets any colder than that, I just don't play), but I love the game. And all four members of my team won one of these bowls in a tournament where we competed with lots of outstanding golfers and various high-profile professional athletes. Did I mention it says "Champion"?

I've got a few other things here  that I think might impress you: my college diploma that says I'm a smart guy (*laude* something, in fact). On the bottom shelf is a plaque that represents an award I got from that same college a few years back—basically says I'm getting smarter all the time and I'm, like, really, really good at what I do. It's right next to my first book, *Humility: How I Achieved It*.

And did you notice this blue thing recharging on my desk? It's called a BlackBerry, and if you're important, you no doubt have one too. Now that I have this, anybody in the world can get a hold of me at any time. I can be text-messaged, emailed, voice-mailed, paged, and calendared. We important types need to be accessible at all times, you understand.

Do you remember when pagers were all the rage? It seemed like everyone who was anyone was wearing one on his belt—well, everyone except for me, that is. I was playing in this softball tournament for a whole weekend with all these guys who had pagers on the belts of their shorts—just in case they had to be reached right away. I felt so out of it and so unimportant that I went out to my truck, got my garage door opener from the visor, and put it on my belt. No kidding!

I mean, we've got to work the image, don't we? Got to make people think we're somebody, right? I think we all fall into that trap. I hate it when I do.

If you want to see image management at its schmooziest (I doubt that's actually a word, but you know what I'm saying), go to a twenty-year reunion. Go to a thirty-year reunion. And just watch everybody trying to impress each other. It's all about working the image.

Here comes the guy who was voted "least likely to succeed" (a prophecy that was fulfilled), and he's thinking, "I'll show them." He's rented a car, a really nice car, and he acts like it's his. He's rented a really nice suit, and he acts like it's his. He's rented a really nice date, and he acts like it's his. Even rented himself some really nice hair. And wishes it were his.

It's true, isn't it, that most of us don't think we look as old as other people our age? I heard about this woman who goes back to her hometown for her fiftieth class reunion. When she gets to the hotel ballroom and sees all these old people sitting around, she thinks to herself, "This can't possibly be the right room." So she asks this old wrinkled guy, "Excuse me, but is this the class of 1957?" He replies, "Why, yes it is."

"Well, I guess this is my class after all, then," she says.

"Really?" he asks. "What subject did you teach?"

The truth is that when we're out there working the image, someone will usually come along and put us in our place. On the cover of my first book, which was actually titled *Making Ripples*, the publisher wrote, "Mike Breaux doesn't do life halfway." Made my family crack up—they about died laughing when they read that.

My wife Debbie started pointing to stuff around the house: "Look at the crown molding," she said. "That's about half done. The deck's about half done too ... and this is half done and that is half done ..." (I won't bore you with the details). My sons Derrick and Drew joined in with a list of dozens of other things I've done "halfway" in my life, and my daughter Jodi started rolling on the couch in laughter, holding the book above her head and saying, "It only took you ten years to finish this one little book. Yeah, Mike Breaux never does anything halfway!"

Shut up you ... you ... stupid family. I'm an *author*!

THAT'S MY BOY ...
THAT'S MY GIRL

You know, image management is always there, just waiting for its cue to activate. We all have at least a little insecurity in us that says, "Look at me. Notice me. I'm important. I'm somebody. I've made it." And the thing is, God put within us the drive to be somebody. He placed within us the passion to excel. He created our healthy ambition, and it's perfectly okay to feel a deep sense of satisfaction over a job well done or some recognition that comes our way.

God wants us to be successful. It's just that his definition of success and the world's definition of success are very different.

Do you know how early in life the world's definition begins? Just visit your local playground sometime and eavesdrop on the conversations of the parents sitting around watching their toddlers play.

You'll hear things like, "So when did she learn to walk?"

"Eleven months."

"Oh, really? Mine walked at three weeks."

"When did she begin to talk?"

"Can he say his ABCs?"

"Well, if he's going to get a scholarship, he'll really need to ..."

There is some pretty ambitious conversation taking place out there on behalf of three-year-olds.

> God wants us to be successful.
> It's just that his definition
> of success and the world's definition
> of success are very different.

For most of my life, I've had the privilege to coach kids in various sports. I love kids. And if left to them, youth sports would be the most fun, most healthy thing on the planet. But enter the parents.

Sit in the stands sometime and listen to and watch those moms and dads who're trying to create a little success for themselves through their kids. They're almost embarrassed by their child's, well, childlikeness. If their son or daughter makes an error, strikes out, shoots an air ball, kicks the ball into the wrong goal, whatever, they go nuts.

I could tell you lots of stories from my coaching days, but one especially comes to mind. We were in the midst of a Little League game, when this kid from the opposing team comes up to the plate. He's a really sweet little boy with a kind spirit, but since he's bigger than most ten-year-olds, expectations run high. He strikes out frequently, and his dad yells at him a lot. On this day, though, he steps up and slams the first pitch over the center field fence for a home run. Everyone goes crazy. Even I, the opposing coach, couldn't help but feel great and cheer for this kid.

As this boy rounds first, his dad, who is coaching first base, yells out so everyone can hear, "It's about #$*%! time!" I wanted to cry. (Then I wanted to punch this guy. Just being honest—it broke my heart.)

A buddy of mine called recently, after his son had played in the eleven-year-old-and-under division of the national AAU basketball tournament. He told me how a game had gotten completely out of control when one of the star players was ejected after getting two technical fouls for mouthing off to the referee. But that wasn't even the worst of it. As soon as the ref makes the call, this kid's mother storms the court, yelling at the top of her lungs, "You can't do that. He's my *franchise*!"

Can you imagine being tagged as a "franchise" when you're eleven years old? By your mom?

And it's not just in sports where this kind of thing happens. In an academic environment marked by the explosion of technology and the fact that human knowledge more than doubles every two years, there's enormous pressure put on school kids to perform. In fact, a recent *Newsweek* article titled "The New First Grade: Too Much Too Soon?" devoted nearly a dozen pages to the fact that, in their words, "In the last decade, the earliest years of schooling have become less like a trip to *Mister Rogers' Neighborhood* and more like SAT prep."

The story reported concerns expressed by parents, teachers, and child-development experts on the constant testing of kids as young as six. And it pointed out that with so much pressure so early, kids can tend to burn out—*by third grade.*

Still, plenty of parents stay preoccupied with their offspring's success. An elementary school principal cited in the article recalls one dad who wanted to know how his son stacked up against his classmates. "I told him we didn't do class ranking in kindergarten," the principal said. But that didn't end the discussion. "If they did do rankings," the dad asked, "would the boy be in the top ten?"

Class ranks. Honor societies. GPAs. Now, don't get me wrong—you ought to do well in school. In fact, you ought to *excel* in school, because it honors God when you do what you know is your very best. And I really do like to see those bumper stickers that say, "I'm the proud parent of an honor student." But I'm also dying to see one that reads, "My kid did his best, got a C, and I'm proud." Or maybe, "My kid has a learning disorder, but he's really, really kind."

Alanis Morissette sings a song called "Perfect," which is written from the perspective of parents talking to their child, pushing him to be what the parents never were; to accomplish what the parents never accomplished. The parents encourage their son to be a good boy and to achieve more to make them happy because, "We'll love you just the way you are ... if you're perfect."

And so the message is sent: When the bell goes off; when the starter pistol fires, do whatever it takes, *whatever* it takes, to blow by your classmates, your coworkers, your teammates, your family, your neighbors. Be bigger. Be smarter. Be stronger. Be faster. Be richer. Be higher. Be better than everyone else.

Remember that guy we talked about in the opening pages of this book—the guy named Solomon? He was the one who tried to cram all the square pegs of this world into the round hole in his heart. The one who said, "What a person desires is unfailing love." Look what the same guy wrote in Ecclesiastes 4:4: "Then I observed that most people are motivated to success by their envy of their neighbors. [Imagine that!] But this, too, is meaningless, like chasing the wind."

What makes us run so fast? What makes us work so hard and compete so intensely? Again, part of it has to do with the God-given drives within us—and channeled in a healthy way, those drives can help us get the most out of life. As I look around, though, I see way too many people whose success-related drives are way out of balance and completely out of control. And I think that's more than a simple desire for success. I think it's a hunger for acceptance. I think it's a longing for the elusive "Atta boy" or "That's my girl." I think it's yet another way some people try to satisfy their hunger for unfailing love.

WOULD SOMEBODY PLEASE LOVE ME?

In my experience, I've found that most workaholics grew up in homes that were pretty much performance driven; where they were taught as little children that love and acceptance are earned. And because the love-need in kids is so strong, if they have to perform, produce, compete, excel, and climb to get acceptance and approval, that's exactly what they'll do.

Fast forward and you'll find that boy or girl has become an adult who is still producing, striving, and performing to hear, in their adult years, what they so seldom heard growing up: "You are loved. You are appreciated. You are so special. You are brilliant. You are good. You are important. I am so proud of you."

Their starvation for unconditional love can produce a perpetual message that plays in their mind, one that goes something like this: *I feel like a nobody and I hate that feeling. I am going to be somebody, and I'm gonna prove that to everyone. I don't care if it takes long hours, or even if it takes seven days a week. It doesn't matter if it costs me my health, my marriage, my relationship with my kids, or even my very soul. I will pay whatever price is necessary, because I can't stand feeling like a loser. I will compete, claw, perform, produce, earn, accumulate, strive, drive, and win until I am appreciated. Until I am accepted. Until I am admired. Until I am finally somebody.*

And this kind of overpowering need to impress others complicates their lives. They can't say no because they crave feeling "in demand." They love to feel indispensable, so they overextend themselves, getting involved in all kinds of projects and causes (often good ones) and spreading themselves incredibly thin. But most of the time they are motivated, not by their personal passion for the cause, but by the fear of not living up to someone else's expectations. Subconsciously, they're saying, *I don't care how frayed and frazzled my life becomes, because I will be liked. I will be admired. I will be accepted, respected, and loved. I will win.*

An elderly friend of mine used to say, "Boy, if you're burnin' the candle at both ends, you're not as bright as you think you are." He's right, you know. It's dumb. But stupid is as stupid does.

Many years ago, I heard a story about a steamboat race on the Mississippi River. These two paddleboats were carrying cargo down the river along the same stretch of water, and the competitive juices of the two crews began to flow. The "battle of the paddles" was on! They started racing down the river, throwing coal on their fires to make more steam. One boat would edge in front of the other; then the other would inch into the lead.

Just as one of the boats was about to take the lead for good, it ran out of coal. So you know what that crew did? Lost in the heat of competition, they began to throw their cargo into the fire, stoking the flames and building the steam. They did indeed pull ahead, leaving the other boat in their wake. (You

can almost hear them yelling, "Eat my steam!")
They won their race. They burned up all their cargo
in the process, you understand. But they won their
race.

Now, please hear this from an extremely fallible
dad, who has battled his own workaholic tendencies
and an out-of-control competitive spirit. Moms,
dads, you know, don't you, that God has entrusted
each of us with extremely precious cargo. I think
all of us might pause here to ask ourselves this
question: Just how much of my precious cargo has
to be burned up in order for me to feel like I'm
winning, to feel like I'm somebody?

I guarantee you that somewhere out there is a
kid who is reading this and crying deep within,
"God, please help my dad see this. Please help my
mom understand what this guy is trying to tell her."
Likewise, there is a spouse right now with a knot in
his or her stomach, saying, "If only I could get my
wife to realize this. If only this could get through to
my husband."

> I don't have to be *the* best;
> I just want to be *my* best —
> to the glory of God.

Remember that blue and red Tupperware ball, the one that's sitting on my office shelf? I told you earlier that I keep this toy in my office to remind me how many empty, frustrated people there are in this world. Well, now I want to tell you the second reason I keep it: to remind me how empty and frustrated I was when I was a workaholic. It takes me back to a time when I tried to cram all that success stuff, all that image stuff into the round hole in my heart. It's a constant reminder that I never want to go back to that place again—and that I don't have to, because the love of Jesus Christ was the perfect fit to fill up that heart hole.

I'm already accepted. I'm already somebody. I don't have to strive or perform. I don't need to keep a crazy schedule so people will like me. God already likes me—with an unfailing like. So I don't have to be rewarded, regarded, or recognized. I don't have to be *the* best; I just want to be *my* best—to the glory of God.

So I keep the toy on my shelf as a reminder that trying to fill up the hole in my heart with anything other than the unfailing love of God will not only frustrate me, but will also frustrate those closest to me. I want to be filled with the unconditional love of God so I'll have something of real value to pass along to my family.

What will you leave behind? When all is said and done, what will your legacy be? If it's based on a nice portfolio, an assortment of plaques and awards, and a thousand lost golf balls, you've kind of missed the point, haven't you? You may have worked the image and you may have looked successful, but you never really loved and you never really lived.

THE SPIN CYCLE

Someone once told me, "Failure is to succeed at something that doesn't really matter." I've never forgotten that. We have to figure out what matters most and then go after that.

I think that's why, when God compiled the original Top Ten list, he put these two commandments at the very top: (1) "Do not worship any other gods besides me," and (2) "Do not make idols of any kind, whether in the shape of birds or animals or fish. You must never worship or bow down to them, for I, the LORD your God, am a jealous God who will not share your affection with any other god!" (Ex. 20:3–5).

Here's how I think this world's definition of success works:

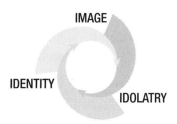

IMAGE

IDENTITY

IDOLATRY

We start with an *image*. Our culture paints a picture for us of what a successful life looks like. Then to put ourselves into that picture, we strive to have the right look, the right clothes, the right car, and the right home in the right neighborhood. We need to go to the right school, so we can get the right job, achieve the right position, make the right salary, and hang with the right group. All that, in turn, enhances the right image.

So we buy in and start chasing this self-made image (a better word might be "mirage") of success. And as we run after it, we find it consumes more and more of our life. I know I'm not overstating this, because I've been there—in a place where all my energies, my time, my affection, my attention, my resources, and my thoughts were set on the pursuit of that image.

Do you know what the Bible calls such pursuit? Worship. When we pour everything we have to give into something, we worship it. And when we worship anything but God, the Bible calls that *idolatry.*

If living life in that way sounds uncomfortably familiar, you're hardly alone. The other night I was watching an episode of *The Apprentice* — reality TV at its cutthroat best. All of these eager, driven young men and women competing to hear Donald Trump say, "You're hired," as they offer viewers a pretty intriguing look into leadership styles, manipulation, alliances, image management, and survival of the fittest. On the episode I watched, one guy who knew he was about to hear the dreaded, "You're fired!" began begging for his corporate life: "I will do anything to work for you, Mr. Trump. Anything. This is my whole life. I've dreamed of this opportunity every day for the last year. I'm consumed with this. I've given every ounce of energy for this. There's nothing else I want to do with my life. I will do anything. *Please …*" The groveling went on and on and on.

I thought, "Anything? Your whole life?" When you'll do absolutely anything for something or someone, that's what has your total allegiance. When you're willing to give every ounce of energy to something, your whole life to it, when you are consumed by the opportunity, then that thing or that someone has your heart and your soul. That's worship.

As I look around our culture, I see millions of people worshiping such an image, trying to attain this image, bowing before this image, and giving the pursuit of this image everything they've got. And the really sad thing is that, in doing so, this image becomes their *identity*.

That's bad news. Because when your identity is all wrapped up in worship of the image, you start to morph into an envious, hyper-competitive, self-absorbed, stressed-out, insecure, approval-seeking person. Then when everything comes crashing down—and it will—you have no idea who you even are. That's because you never really got to know who God is. You directed your worship toward other gods, and those "little-*g*" gods are not only unworthy of your worship, but they can do absolutely nothing to help with the huge gaping hole still left in your heart.

In Luke 18, we meet a young guy in the spin cycle of identity theft, thanks to his commitment to keep up the image.

From all appearances, this is one dude who has it together. Abercrombie toga. K-Swiss on his feet. Young and hip, he could be the cover boy for *Mediterranean* GQ. He's speed dating at the Jerusalem Club and driving a pimped-out chariot with all the options, including a moon roof. Most people in the crowd figure this is a guy who has life all figured out, but in reality, the image leaves him empty. So he looks up this rabbi, this teacher named Jesus, and sensing maybe there is more to life than mere image, he asks, "Good teacher, what must I do to inherit eternal life?" (Luke 18:18 NIV).

We've all had these kinds of questions, haven't we? What happens when I die? Is this all there is? Will I go to heaven? There is a fundamental problem, though, with the question this young man asks. Think about it: what did you have to do to get written into your parents' will? Nothing. You cannot *earn* an inheritance; you are simply granted it, based on your relationship with the giver.

But because this guy is a peak performer, a high achiever in areas ranging from finance to religion, he figures, "I've always had to *do* something." So he asks Jesus, "What must I *do*?"

A lot of us, like this guy, are convinced that our eternal destiny is a result of our earthly behavior. Doing good and living right should be a response to a loving God, but it is *not* a performance plan that merits eternal life. That's a gift from the Father through his Son's sacrifice on a blood-stained cross, what many people describe as amazing grace.

I think we can all understand, though, why this guy feels the way he does. He is very successful. He is very wealthy. In his Hebrew culture, people like him were viewed as especially accepted and blessed by God. So he's working the success image and assumes he has worked his way into God's favor.

> Doing good and living right
> should be a response
> to a loving God,
> but it is *not* a performance plan
> that merits eternal life.

Jesus asks him: "Been following the rules? Kept all the commandments—you know, do not commit adultery, do not murder, do not steal, do not give false testimony, honor your father and mother ...?" It's no accident that as Jesus clicks off these commandments, he omits the first two—the ones about "no other gods" and "no bowing down to images" that have to do with a personal, intimate relationship with God. Instead, he lists the outward commands—the ones people can see, the ones that help reinforce the image.

"All these I have kept since I was a boy," the young man answers (Luke 18:21 NIV). Can't you just sense his pride? Not *some* of those commandments, but *all* of them. Not just now, but *since I was a boy.* "I've got a 4.0! I'm looking good!"

Truth is, he probably had no clue about his self-deception. Because when you live with a compulsive desire to present a perfect image—so everybody will admire you—the result is that nobody will ever actually *know* you. You won't even know yourself.

But God knows the real you. He knows your true self.

The book of Mark tells us that Jesus looked at this young man and loved him. Isn't that cool? Although he could see right through the façade this image-chasing guy was putting forth, Jesus loved him. "You're a good guy," he seems to be saying. "You've never broken any of the commandments, at least you think you haven't. You're really trying to do the right thing." Being a good guy and trying hard, though, do not address the worship question. In fact, they can be their own form of idolatry.

" 'One thing you lack,' [Jesus] said. 'Go, sell everything you have and give to the poor, and you will have treasure in heaven. Then come, follow me.' At this the man's face fell. He went away sad, because he had great wealth" (Mark 10:21–22 TNIV).

"You're bowing down before the wrong image," Jesus was saying. "You look like you have it all, but you lack surrender to the unfailing love of the true and living God. Get to know him; put him first in your life. Because right now, God doesn't really have your heart, does he? He doesn't have your affections. And until he does, you won't really know yourself. Until you have that one thing right in your life, it will keep you from living a real life on this side—and on the other side—of eternity."

Let's make one thing clear. The issue here was not this guy's money. A person can be poor and be just as empty and lost as he was. I have great friends who have lots of money and love God with all their hearts. They are generous with the poor and are always using what God has blessed them with to help others. It's not an economic issue. It's a heart issue. Who or what has it? This young man's image, his possessions, his success, had his heart and had stolen his worship. And in the process, this image also stole his identity.

FIRST THINGS FIRST

I think God takes a different approach to this whole success deal—that in his economy, in his view of success, our first priority is to get this one right: we've got to put *identity* at the top.

IDENTITY

IMAGE

INTIMACY

When you begin to know who God is and who you are in his eyes—when you renew your mind with that truth—your *identity* becomes settled. It becomes certain. You are a much-loved child of God. You have a God who is perfect, pure, strong, wise, loving, faithful—and he wants to do awesome, eternal things with your life. That identity is the starting point for everything else, so it's extremely important to get this one nailed down first.

Once this first piece is in place, you can move toward *intimacy*—with God and with other people. Because when you truly know who you are, when you're secure and accepted as a treasured child of God, you'll be on your way to really knowing him and the things that make his heart beat fast (one of which is *you*!). And as that intimacy begins to flow between you and God, it enhances the intimacy between you and your spouse, between you and your kids. In fact, you'll start bringing a more secure, joy-filled person into all your relationships.

You have a God
who is perfect, pure, strong,
wise, loving, faithful —
and he wants to do awesome,
eternal things with your life.

Then where does such intimacy lead? To the accurate *image*. Because instead of bowing to some phony, wannabe god, you now start to reflect the image of your Creator. You begin to live in the image of God again, just as he always intended.

With all due respect to *The Lion King*, this is the true circle of life — a life-*giving* circle that moves from *identity* to *intimacy* to *image*. When you know who God is, and who you really are in his eyes; when you're intimate with God and getting to know his character and experiencing his love; then you start to reflect the image of God through the way you live your life. And that, my friend, is why we were created.

I cannot tell you how passionate I am about this. It's the whole ballgame. It's your *life*! So as we take a closer look at each of the components along our new circle, it is imperative that we begin with identity. Because the extent to which you really know who God is and what he says about you sets up your life for success or failure.

The key to learning is repetition. The key to learning is repetition. The key to learning is repetition. The key ... alright! I know you've already seen the following Scripture several times by now, but I want you to read it again. (Or, if you're one of those very conscientious readers who have already memorized it, just close your eyes for a minute and say it out loud.) Actually, regardless of whether or not you've got it memorized, it would be great if you would say these words out loud:

> *And I pray that Christ will be more and more at home in your hearts as you trust in him. May your roots go down deep into the soil of God's marvelous love. And may you have the power to understand [grasp], as all God's people should, how wide, how long, how high, and how deep his love really is. May you experience the love of Christ, though it is so great you will never fully understand it. Then you will be filled with the fullness of life and power that comes from God. (Ephesians 3:17 – 19)*

Grasp it. Know it. Be captured by it. I love how the internationally respected Benedictine monk Bede Griffiths once put it: "The love of God is not a mild benevolence; it's a consuming power."

This God we're talking about is a God who has a passionate, raging, consuming love for you. He loves you so much he sent the only Son he ever had, wrapped in our skin. That Son learned to walk. He stumbled and fell. He cried out for milk, for his mom, for his dad. He sweated blood in the night, was lashed with a whip and showered with spit. He was nailed to a cross, and he died whispering forgiveness on us all. Grasp that! Let that consume

you. Be captured by the high, wide, long, deep love
God has for you.

I realize that's a struggle for some people. If you
grew up thinking God is this loose cannon, just
kind of firing random shots at screwups like us,
you're likely to be fear motivated. You're probably
performance driven or an approval addict who
may well be unbending and unrealistic in your
expectations of other people.

> This God we're talking about
> is a God who has a passionate,
> raging, consuming love for you.

In order to accept God's true identity, you may
have to work at specifically setting aside this narrow,
punitive picture of him. As you are able to trust in
the God who loves you consistently and freely, it
will change you. A loving God fosters loving people.
I believe that because our view of God's identity
shapes our own identity so profoundly, this may be
one of the reasons Scripture invites us over and over
again to *be still*. "Be still, and know that I am God"
(Psalm 46:10 NIV). Get to know God. Get this
identity thing right. It's time.

Sometimes people resist that invitation. They'll
say, "Bro, I hear what you're saying, but I have a hard

time seeing God like that." They tell me about their parents or maybe some pastor in the church where they grew up, who somehow hid the true identity of the God of unfailing love. Instead, they painted a picture of a distant, out-of-touch God who, when he did get involved, just threw down judgment and wrath.

Let me say this with as much grace as I possibly can. It's time to stop blaming everyone else and to experience God yourself. *You* dig in and learn what he says and what he's like. *You* get to know the truth about who he is and the truth about who you are in his eyes. Yes, the process will require some work. It can take time, after all, to erase the faulty negative images you've carried around for so long. It may even take reaching out for the help of a Christian who'll act as a spiritual mentor—someone to help keep you on track and to celebrate your progress. But the potential results of your efforts are impossible to overestimate. And the only drawback will be the number of times you'll ask yourself, "What on earth took me so long to get started?"

TITLES AND SUCH

I love Brennan Manning's book *Abba's Child*. It's a great read, and I especially enjoy this description of God's love:

> The God who flung from his fingerprints this universe filled with galaxies and stars, penguins and puffins, gulls and gannets, Pomeranians and poodles, elephants and evergreens, parrots and potato bugs, peaches and pears, and a world full of children made in his image, is the God who loves with magnificent monotony.

Monotony? Anyone who has experienced God's love will tell you the synonym for monotony is not "boring." Instead, it means the same thing again and again and again. It's radical. It's consuming. It's unfailing. And it's constant.

When I grasp the deep, deep love of God for me; when I embrace the truth that God accepts me, just as I am, through Jesus Christ; when my eyes are open and my heart is pierced by the truth, I can finally accept myself. That kind of self-acceptance is not available through the power of positive thinking. We cannot achieve it through reading volumes of self-help books. It comes from an act of faith in the God of grace who made me—who made you.

Does self-acceptance mean we no longer strive? Does it mean we're resigned to live a mediocre, non-excellent, non-productive, non-passionate, non-ambitious kind of life? No, quite the opposite. When you really know who you are; when you grasp that you are accepted; when you walk with the confidence that you are secure; when the realization that you are significant in the eyes of God begins to build intimacy with him—all that frees you up to be the best you have ever been. It enables you to bring a whole new level of passion and excellence to your job, your schoolwork, your ministry, and your relationships.

That's because as you get to know God and understand where his heart is, your own heart starts to beat after the same things. Life begins to make sense, and purpose starts to surge through your veins. And as your intimacy with God grows, things like love, joy, peace, patience, kindness, and goodness begin to replace the envy, selfish ambition, insecurity, and attention-seeking behavior that you developed out there on your own.

The truth is, when you embrace your true identity as a child of God, you decrease your hunger for power and your appetite for stuff. You're thankful for your life. You deeply appreciate love, and one of the results of your intimacy with God is that you begin to love yourself. You no longer seek the applause of the crowd, and the opinions of others can no longer hold you captive. After all, you've already been accepted by the One who matters most.

WHAT'S YOUR TITLE?

Lots of people in the corporate world get really caught up in titles. What am I going to be called? What's my title? Am I a senior vice president? Am I the vice president's executive assistant? Does my title reflect how very, very important I am to this organization?

Thank goodness no one who works in a church ever worries over such things. *Yeah, right!* You wouldn't believe the arguments church staff members can get into over what they're going to be called. In fact, I don't know why I've kept it, but I've got this sign here that I ripped off the door of my office in a church where I worked thirty years ago. Here's what it says. [Note to reader: please read the following title aloud in your deepest, most impressive voice.]

Mike Breaux, Minister to Youth

Well, at the time, I thought it was very impressive.

I went on to be called senior pastor for a number of years, but when I arrived at my current church in suburban Chicago, that no longer fit. I had been asked to assume kind of a unique role, so they also asked me, "What do you want us to call you?"

"I don't know—Bro would be fine," I said.

"No, what *title* do you prefer?" they insisted.

"Uh, I don't know. Senior pastor is already taken, so how about associate? No, wait a minute, I'm not sure how you guys might abbreviate that. Whatever you decide; it really doesn't matter."

So after I convinced them I just really didn't give a rip about what title was in front of my name, someone decided on teaching pastor, which is just fine with me.

I have thought, though, that there is one description that would be cooler. You know how sometimes when you put on a pair of jeans you haven't worn in a long time and you reach in the pocket about halfway through the day and there's twenty bucks in there? You go, "Whoa, man, that's awesome!" Well, sometimes reading Scripture is like that for me.

An example of that is an obscure verse I happened on in the middle of a story. It says, "Peter turned and saw that the disciple whom Jesus loved was following them" (John 21:20 NIV).

Now check this out real quick. Do you know who was called the disciple Jesus loved? It was John. And did you see who wrote that verse? John. I think that's cool. John could have said, "John, the apostle," "John, associate disciple," "John, minister to youth." But instead he says, "Hey, I'm just the one Jesus loves." That was his only title.

And you know what? That's the only title I need, too. It's the only title you need. You are deeply loved by God. Define yourself as someone who's just radically loved by God. That's your true identity; every other identity is just an illusion.

Can I get you to read out loud just one more time? Repeat after me:

My worth is not found in my possessions. My worth is not found in my reputation. My worth is not found in my title. My worth is not found in "Atta boys" or headlines or trophies or everyone telling me how important I am to the organization. I stand anchored in the love of God—the deep, wide, high, long love of God, the one who tells me, "Hey, you're my kid and I love you with a radical love." And that's all I need to be.

Feel free to mark this page so you can come back and repeat that paragraph as often as you need to.

Define yourself as someone
who's just radically loved by God.
That's your true identity;
every other identity is just an illusion.

The Bible says, "Draw close to God, and God will draw close to you." When you begin to experience intimacy with God, you start changing. Your identity starts changing. Your image starts changing. You no longer want to project the image you used to work so hard at protecting, because it feels so free to be the person God intended you to be.

SUCCESS RE-IMAGINED

There was a guy named Saul who was a "work-the-image" kind of guy. He was rich, successful, intelligent, powerful, respected, and admired—yet he lacked one thing. He, too, was empty inside. And then he met Jesus Christ. He became a whole new person; in fact, he even changed his name to Paul. And he wrote about half of the New Testament.

One of the greatest transitional paragraphs in all of Scripture is found in Philippians 3:7–9. You'll really want to sit down and read Philippians 3 in its entirety sometime. For now, though, let me share just this portion:

I once thought all these things [all this status, all this success I had] were so very important, but now I consider them worthless because of what Christ has done. Yes, everything else is worthless when compared with the priceless gain of knowing Christ Jesus my Lord. I have discarded everything else, counting it all as garbage, so that I may have Christ and become one with him. (Philippians 3:7–9)

Paul is saying, "You know what? I'm done with impressing people. I'm done with working the image. I'm done with chasing the dream." And if you can personally say that (and mean it) too, it's a good day. Because all the energy you used to expend chasing the image and trying to work that whole deal can now be poured into stuff that really, really matters. Which is, after all, the true meaning of success.

We sure can get hung up, sometimes, about the definition of that word. My mom wanted so badly for me to be a doctor. Now, being a physician is an extremely noble profession, but I would have been the worst doctor in the history of the world. I hate the sight of blood. I've literally passed out on hospital visits as I tried to cheer up patients! It's awful. I'm a needle-fearing, catheter-fleeing, hospital wimp.

But my mom wanted me to be a doctor, because my mom wanted me to be somebody. See, she never had much growing up. And my mom (who is now in heaven with more than she ever dreamed) had really low self-esteem. She was a great woman, but it took her a long time before she really grasped how high and wide and deep and long the love of God was for her. So she was always pushing me to be someone important, which would, in turn, make her feel important.

Well, she was crushed when I decided to go to a Christian Bible college to become Mike Breaux, minister to youth.

One day, a few weeks before graduation, I remember standing in front of the college bookstore, looking at this bulletin board. Next to the "I need a ride home to Arizona" and "Beanbag chair for sale" postings, there was a list from a magazine article that ranked the prestige factor of lots of occupations. Americans had been surveyed, and out of a possible sixty points, "doctor" earned fifty-nine, putting it at the top of the list. (Mom was right!) Number two on the list was lawyer; number three was the president of the United States; number four was professional athlete. And so on down the list.

At the time, I was twenty years old, just married, working three part-time jobs, and going to school. I was curious about where my jobs had landed on the survey. Let's see, I was a janitor at a local grade school. So I'm scanning the list—custodian, custodian, janitor, janitor. Ah, there it is, close to the bottom of the list with ten points.

I thought, "Maybe my other job's a little more prestigious." I was a dockworker at the co-op feed mill, where I loaded semi-trailers and farm trucks. I mean, you had to be strong and in good shape to do that. So I'm looking for dockworker, dockworker, and there it was, tied with janitor at ten points.

Alright, I thought, my third job surely will be higher than that. I was a gas station attendant—and not at some pay-at-the-pump deal, either. I was a *full-service* gas attendant with an embroidered name on my Phillips 66 shirt! But there was gas station attendant, right down there at the bottom with the other two.

Well, my pride started acting up, and I thought, "Wait a minute! In just a few months, I'll graduate from college. Then I'm going to be a full-fledged minister!" Scanning. Scanning. Still scanning. Minister didn't even make the list!

Do you know what I've learned in my lifetime? That there is nothing more prestigious than to be used by God in your life, no matter what your occupation may be.

Your prestige comes from the fact that you are fearfully and wonderfully made in the image of God. You are just someone Jesus loves. If you're a doctor, do your work with the knowledge that you are already somebody—somebody with a sharp mind and incredible gifts that come from a God who wants to use you in this unique way. If you're a teacher, do your work because that's where God has placed you to make a difference in this world. If you're a gas station attendant, a carpenter, a nurse, a dentist, a computer geek, a truck driver, a janitor, or a dockworker, do your work because that's where God placed you to create some "ripples" with your life—some positive influence and impact that will still be felt long after you are dead and gone.

> Your prestige comes from
> the fact that you are fearfully
> and wonderfully made
> in the image of God.

That's success! That's a prestigious existence. That's where you stand back, deeply satisfied, and say, "Wow, God, I never imagined this! Thanks so much for using my life in this way."

After years of chasing my own version of the American dream, I decided I would rather chase after *God's* dream for my life. My appetite for notoriety, wealth, comfort, trophies, and titles was greatly diminished. My worth stopped depending on a paycheck, a corner office, a résumé, or a mirror. I'm a little uncertain about those things that make up my 401(k), but I know for sure I want to stuff things like love, joy, peace, patience, kindness, goodness, faithfulness, gentleness, and self-control into my portfolio. And the Holy Spirit of God is making that eternal investment happen.

The identity thief comes to kill, steal, and destroy. Jesus came that we might have life to the full. This life is sweet and rich; not always easy, but deeply satisfying.

Hey, thanks for stopping by my office today, and before you leave, there's one more thing I'd like to tell you. I keep this little clay man my son Drew made when he was in first grade. He fashioned it in such a way that the guy is on his knees with his hands raised to God in worship. It's a great sculpture. No spectacular work of art, but just a little kneeling guy molded into shape by a six-year-old. I keep it on the middle shelf of my bookcase, to remind me every day who I worship and who I really am.

Just like you, I was made to reflect the image of God, rather than to devote my energies to work or worship on my own. That's what I want to do with my one and only life. Don't you? Because failure is to succeed at something that doesn't really matter.

4

PICKPOCKETED BY THE PAST

Someone at work gave me a piece of Dubble Bubble the other day, and it was amazing how the taste and elasticity of that gum transported me back in time. As soon as it hit my mouth, I was back in Little League as a ten-year-old baseball player. I was chomping away as I walked down the hall, imagining myself back in the dugout, knocking dirt off my cleats in the on-deck circle, and taking swings at the plate.

Then the minute I turned the corner into my office (the one you just toured), I spotted it there on the third shelf from the bottom: my very first baseball mitt. I slipped it on, blew a huge bubble, and pounded my hand into the pocket of that old glove. It was one of those smile-deep-inside moments as I remembered the sound of the crowd, the mingled smells of hot dogs, popcorn, and Fudgsicles coming from the concession stand, and the sight of the red brick school building just beyond the left-field fence.

I recently went back and visited my old elementary school—and what a flood of memories *that* created. Gone were the old wooden desks—you know, the kind you could carve your name into with the sharp end of a compass. I can remember carving MB + KL. I had a big-time crush on Kathy—man, was she cute! I chased her around at recess, put tacks on her seat, and pulled her pigtails. (In fifth grade, you express your affection in some pretty strange ways.)

When I glanced into my sixth-grade classroom, I noticed that the chalkboard where I had written "I will not throw spit wads" a hundred times had been replaced with a white dry-erase board. And PCs were lined up on the counter where the radio always sat. Mrs. Cole used to tune that old AM dial to Paul Harvey every day at noon, and our class would listen as he'd say, "Hello, Americans, this is Paul Harvey. Stand by—for news." I remembered the sound of his voice like it was yesterday.

I know, I know. I'm sounding really old right now—kind of like the Rolling Stones might feel on their "I Can't Get No Circulation" Tour. But I'm a bit nostalgic as I flash back over my seventeen years of formal education. And I'm smiling as I think of all the crazy things I did, but never got caught at.

Except for this one time. When my buddy Greg and I were high-school sophomores, we decided to climb up through the drop ceiling of our classroom, scale the dividing partition, and drop through the ceiling of the classroom next door. When our chemistry teacher stepped out of the room, we took off like characters from the *Shawshank Redemption*. Greg got up through the tiles first and was into the rafters, but I was still dangling from the top of the wall when our teacher walked back in. She looked up and yelled, "Mr. Breaux, *what are you doing?*"

I didn't know what to say, except, "Uh, I'm looking for Greg." Just about then, he was dropping through the ceiling of the classroom next door. We got in so much trouble!

That memory doesn't embarrass me near as much, though, as my recollections surrounding Robert and Wanda, a couple kids my friends and I considered a little "different." As I think of them now, I get a knot in my stomach and am filled with more than a little regret—the memory of how I treated them makes me wish I could roll back the clock and be a little different myself. Out of my own teenage insecurity and immaturity, I made fun of them. Gave them unflattering nicknames. Got lots of laughs at their expense. I'm sure it hurt them, and now it hurts me to think about it.

Nicknames have a way of sticking with us, you know? I sure had my share of them growing up, starting in grade school with the name Pee Wee, to reflect the fact that I was a little bitty guy. Later, because my name was Breaux (pronounced Bro, as you'll recall), I was called every variation of Bro-something. Instead of Bozo, I was Brozo. Bromoseltzer. Bromoside. Dodo Bro.

As a seventeen-year-old college freshman, I was not exactly your "early bloomer." I was five foot seven, a hundred and twenty-eight pounds, and really, really skinny. So when I suited up to play freshman basketball, more nicknames started to fly.

This was the era when we played in short white shorts with tube socks pulled up to our knees; in addition, I had long white bandages wrapped around my sore knees. If you also recall that I had tons of flowing hair (this was in the seventies), you'll understand why they tagged me "the human Q-tip."

There was this other guy on campus who was just as skinny as I was. He called me "Stick," and I called him "Stick." Every time we'd walk past each other, I'd nod and go, "Stick." And in return he'd go, "Stick." We continued that all the way through college, until I got married and moved off campus. About six months later, I was walking to class one day and saw him coming toward me. I went, "Stick." He paused, did a double take and said, "Donut." I guess marriage had been good to me.

What about you? What did they call you? Got any nicknames that still kind of mess with you? Does the stuff they used to say about you still affect the way you see yourself? Does it affect the way you live? Can you still hear those voices?

Well, I hope that as you've read this book, you've begun to clearly hear the voice of God telling you what *he* thinks of you. (His voice is, after all, the only one that really matters.) If you haven't, then I hope you will hear him say to you right here and right now, *You are not defined by what they used to call you. You are not defined by the nicknames they shouted at you at recess or the hurtful things your parents used to say about you or the awful thing that someone did to you. They were wrong. You don't have to be paralyzed by that past. You can and you should move on to a new life and a new day and a new identity.*

Of course, maybe it was not so much what was said or done to you. Maybe it's something *you* did that you can't get out of your mind.

Maybe it was a DUI, a failed marriage, or a financial collapse. Maybe you flunked out of school, had sexual experiences you'd rather forget, or got fired from your job. Your past may have included an affair, an abortion, or an addiction. Perhaps you were inmate number 37842 or maybe you spent ten years introducing yourself as "Hi, my name is _____, and I am an alcoholic." Maybe you were not only the victim of abuse, but you grew up to be an abuser. Maybe you were hooked on pornography or gambling. And no matter what it was, maybe what happened back then still defines you today. In fact, maybe it has become who you are.

Just like imperfect relationships, a distorted image in the mirror, and the mirage of success, the past can hack into your soul and do a real number on you. It, too, can steal your identity.

THE MALIGNANCY OF GUILT

Dealing with guilt can be a tricky proposition. When a bunch of kids were asked to explain what a guilty conscience is like, one little girl replied, "A guilty conscience is a pot inside of you that burns if you're not good." Pretty perceptive, wouldn't you say? A seven-year-old boy was a little more pragmatic. "A guilty conscience," he said, "is feeling bad when you kick girls or little dogs."

What they were trying to say is that guilt is that thing inside us that goes, "Whoa. I think I crossed the line there." It's that thing that says, "That wasn't right. That didn't even *feel* right."

Guilt from that perspective can be a good thing. I mean, if you get to the point where you don't feel the little twinge of "that was wrong" in your heart, then your heart is heading toward a cold, callous, and dangerous place. Guilt can lead us to honesty. Guilt can lead us to confession. Guilt can lead us to forgiveness. Guilt can lead us to a better decision the next time around.

Unresolved guilt, however—the kind of guilt that gets suppressed, stuffed down, and hidden—is a really destructive thing.

In his classic story "The Tell-Tale Heart," Edgar Allan Poe's main character has committed murder and is unable to escape the haunting guilt of his dastardly deed. He begins to hear the heartbeat of his victim, whom he has buried in the basement.

The storyteller breaks out in a cold sweat as the thump-thump, thump-thump, thump-thump of his victim's heartbeat relentlessly pounds at him until it drives him insane. Ultimately, of course, it becomes clear that the pounding that drove this killer mad was not the heartbeat of his victim buried in the basement, but of the heart in his own chest. And so it is with unresolved guilt.

In the Bible's Old Testament, King David was the guy who had to deal with the relentless pounding of unconfessed guilt hidden in his chest. He had an affair with a married woman, then tried to cover up the whole mess by having her military husband killed in battle. His unresolved guilt and futile attempts to hide his sin began to eat him alive, until—finally—he took the critical step of getting honest with God.

Look at what he wrote in his prayer to God:

I know how bad I've been; my sins are staring me down. You're the One I've violated, and you've seen it all, seen the full extent of my evil. You have all the facts before you; whatever you decide about me is fair. I've been out of step with you for a long time, in the wrong since before I was born. What you're after is truth from the inside out. Enter me, then; conceive a new, true life. (Psalm 51:3–6 MSG)

You see, David learned a principle that all of us eventually experience, whether we want to acknowledge it or not: secret sin cannot coexist with inner peace. I think that's a principle worth repeating—even worth highlighting, if you're so inclined: *Secret sin cannot coexist with inner peace.*

In his book *Guilt: Where Psychology and Religion Meet*, Dr. David Belgum estimates that 75 percent of the people hospitalized with physical illnesses actually have sickness rooted in emotional problems. He writes, "Their physical symptoms and breakdowns are, for many, their involuntary confessions of guilt."

Unresolved guilt is a malignant kind of thing, capable of spreading and poisoning every part of us. Just look at what else King David had to say on this subject: "When I refused to confess my sin, I was weak and miserable, and I groaned all day long. Day and night your hand of discipline was heavy on me. My strength evaporated like water in the summer heat" (Ps. 32:3–4).

> Unresolved guilt
> is a malignant kind of thing,
> capable of spreading and
> poisoning every part of us.

David admits that physically, mentally, emotionally, and spiritually, the guilt he holds inside is just eating him up. Then he adds a little pause — the word *Selah* in the Hebrew language is a musical signpost indicating an interlude or change. And at this point, there's a new rhythm and intensity as this song prepares to crank things up a notch. Look at what comes next: "Finally, I confessed all my sins to you and stopped trying to hide them. I said to myself, 'I will confess my rebellion to the LORD.' And you forgave me! All my guilt is gone" (Ps. 32:5).

Did you notice what was wiped away right along with the sin? The guilt. That's because the guilt had served its purpose.

My friend Charlie Gerber, who is a counselor in Indiana, showed me his little acrostic on guilt. He says that from God's perspective, guilt is a very good thing; that it is:

God's
Unique
Intentional
Loving
Treatment

In its purest form, guilt is God's unique intentional loving treatment. It's like that "check engine" light on the dashboard of your car that lets you know something's not quite right under the hood. God created the emotion of guilt in us to let us know when something is not quite right inside our hearts. When we feel guilty, it's a clear signal we've got something going on we need to address.

But as you might imagine, Satan takes what God made for good and distorts it. He takes it to the other extreme. Here's the acrostic for guilt from the original identity thief's perspective:

Grief

United

In

Lifelong

Torment

When viewed in this way, guilt fits neatly into Satan's agenda to kill, steal, and destroy. You see, guilt that is left unconfessed, unforgiven, and unresolved eventually morphs into its uglier, more sinister cousin named Shame. Shame takes guilt to a whole new level by attacking your core. And as it does so, it is more than capable of stealing your identity and keeping you paralyzed in the past.

In his book *Facing Shame*, Merle Fossum writes, "A pervasive sense of shame is the ongoing premise that one is fundamentally bad, inadequate, defective, unworthy or not fully valid as a human being."

Author Lewis Smedes takes the description one step further: "The difference between guilt and shame is very clear in theory," he explains. "We feel guilty for what we do. We feel shame for what we are. A person feels guilt because he *did* something wrong. A person feels shame because he *is* something wrong."

Do you see how that can mess with our identity? The Bible not only calls Satan the enemy of our soul, the thief, and the father of lies, but also our *accuser.* Have you heard his accusing whispers? He says things like, "You know who you really are. You are such a loser. You're a drunk. You're an addict. You're a junkie. You're a pervert. You're just stupid. You're so fat. You're plain ugly. You're such a geek. You're unloved. You're so alone—always have been and always will be. Come on, let's just face it— that's just who you *are.*"

Shame is an extremely dangerous enemy.

You need to know, though, that shame has met its match in God's grace. If shame tells me I'm defective, grace counters that I'm valuable. Where shame's greatest weapon is fear of judgment, grace's even greater weapon is the relief of unfailing love.

Shame says that because I'm flawed, I'm unacceptable; grace says that even though I'm flawed, I am priceless. Shame believes that what really matters are other people's opinions; grace counters that God's opinion is the only one that counts. Shame claims I must become perfect to earn approval; grace claims I am accepted regardless of my imperfections. Shame makes us hide; grace sets us free. Shame is the language of the thief. Grace, on the other hand, is the language of Jesus.

Shame says that
because I'm flawed,
I'm unacceptable;
grace says that
even though I'm flawed,
I am priceless.

So you take your guilt, you take your sin, you take your past, and—like David did, like I've done, like countless other people have done—you just get honest with God. You come clean with him no matter what you've been involved in, no matter how far you've strayed, or how dark your life has become. You let his grace and his unfailing love sweep away your shame, restore your soul, and reclaim your identity. I have found that your truth plus God's truth equals freedom.

There's a Scripture I use all the time when I write out my prayers. The reason I journal my prayers, by the way, is because I'm such an airhead that I can start praying and then about thirty seconds later realize I'm thinking about SportsCenter highlights. I've found that writing out my prayers helps me stay focused.

Often I list my specific sinful thoughts, actions, and attitudes—not to inform God (like he would wonder, "Really? When did you do *that*?"), but for my own benefit. I want to regularly check under the hood and get all the sludge out of there. So after I write all these things down, I take a red Sharpie out of the top right drawer of my desk and write over the top of what I've just written, "1 John 1:9. FORGIVEN!"

First John 1:8 says that if we say we don't have any sin in our lives, we're just kidding ourselves. Then look at what verse 9 says: "But if we confess our sins to him, he is faithful and just to forgive us and to cleanse us from every wrong" (1 John 1:9).

I love that verse because it tells me that when I become a Christ-follower and accept the forgiveness and the grace of God, I'm still not going to be perfect. I'll continue to screw up along the way. But when I make mistakes—when I sin, when I fall—I will get honest with myself and with God and confess those sins. And as I do that with humility and sincerity, God will clean me up.

ONE STEP AT A TIME

Ever watch little kids learn to walk? They've got these big heads and big diaper-padded rear ends, combined with these really wobbly legs. When their parents stick out their index fingers, kids grab hold and begin to walk. But as they take several steps, the mom or dad may gently remove their fingers from the toddler's grasp. And all of a sudden, the head's going this way, the rear end's going that way, and boom! They fall right down.

Now what good parent would walk over at that point, kick their fallen child, and yell, "Get up, you stupid kid! You ought to be walking by now!" No one I know. But that's how way too many people think of God—that he's just waiting for us to fall so he can kick us when we're down.

No, like a good father, our Abba, our daddy, God reaches down and says, "Alright, you fell. We both know it. Thanks for being honest with me about that. Let me help you up. I forgive you. Let's go three steps today; four tomorrow; five the next day. I promise I'll be right there helping you walk every day—and that you won't fall nearly as often when we walk together. But when you do stumble, know I love you. Know I will help you up every single time. Because you're my priceless child."

As you learn to believe in the truth of that promise, the Bible says you can reap real benefits by having a trusted friend or group of friends with whom you can also come clean. When you become part of an honest community, you'll discover that most of us are like the rest of us. We all struggle with something. And there's just something very powerful about getting honest with a trustworthy community of like-strugglers. In fact, the Bible says it's a significant key to healing: "Confess your sins to each other and pray for each other so that you may be healed" (James 5:16). God wired us to be in community, and when there is an openness to human frailty among friends, there is a spirit of acceptance and grace that can transform our lives. Together, we can begin to grasp our true identities as much-loved children of God.

I want you to see that Scripture from Ephesians 3 one more time. (Actually, I'm hoping you may have committed it to memory by now.)

> *And I pray that Christ will be more and more at home in your hearts as you trust him. May your roots go down deep into the soil of God's marvelous love. And may you have the power to understand, as all God's people should, how wide, how long, how high, and how deep his love really is. (Ephesians 3:17–18)*

Grasping the truth of that Scripture is the key to your freedom from the past. And it's only the beginning of what God's Word has to say on the subject. Consider the following:

> *I, even I, am he who blots out your transgressions, for my own sake, and remembers your sins no more. (Isaiah 43:25 NIV)*

I have swept away your sins like the morning mists. I have scattered your offenses like the clouds. Oh, return to me, for I have paid the price to set you free. (Isaiah 44:22)

Once again you will have compassion on us. You will trample our sins under your feet and throw them into the depths of the ocean! (Micah 7:19)

He has removed our rebellious acts as far away from us as the east is from the west. (Psalm 103:12 NIV)

I will never again remember their sins and lawless deeds. (Hebrews 10:17)

So now there is no condemnation for those who belong to Christ Jesus. (Romans 8:1)

Those six brief verses are a mere sampling of God's perspective on your past. Know their truth. Grasp their reality. Your truth plus his truth equals healing.

God wired us to be in community,
and when there is
an openness to human frailty
among friends, there is a spirit
of acceptance and grace
that can transform our lives.

THE ETCH A SKETCH GOSPEL

One Christmas, I got three pretty cool toys. Well, two of them were actually fairly lame. One was a Slinky, which would have been okay, but we lived in a ranch-style house. You kinda need stairs for those things.

The second gift was an electric football game. Did you ever play with one of those? I'm not talking about high-tech, high-def, Xbox, PS3, Madden 07 kinds of virtual reality football action. This was a green metal board painted to look like a football field. You set up these little plastic guys, then flipped a switch. The "players" began vibrating and moving all over the board—your running back was heading the wrong direction; your linebackers were square dancing in the corner. It was a pretty worthless game, but it sure did make us laugh!

The third toy I got, though, is a classic. Still have it, of course; in fact, it sits on my office shelf right next to my red and blue Tupperware ball. It is an Etch A Sketch, and I suspect your childhood included one of those as well. I would turn those two little white knobs at the bottom and "draw" for hours. Of course, I was never really able to create anything much more complex than stairs going up or down, but I sure did make a lot of those. Oh sure, I tried to draw everything from a horse to a mountain range, but I mostly just ended up with a lot of squiggly little lines. Mastering an Etch A Sketch is a really hard deal.

But you already know the best part about that toy, don't you? When you mess up, all you have to do is shake it and you get to start all over again! And though it came several years later, it was a good day when I learned to take all my failures and screwups and mistakes and sins to God and hand over my Etch A Sketch life to him. Because I knew he'd shake it and hand it back, saying, "There you go—now start again. My mercies are new every morning."

I doubt you're surprised I keep that toy in my office. It reminds me, every time I see it, that the God of unfailing love does not want me to be defined by the person I used to be. That's exactly what he wants all of us to understand. That's exactly what he wants *you* to understand.

Twenty-seven-year-old Ben, a friend of mine whose life has done a 180, sent me this note awhile back:

Mike—

Hey, I can't believe it's been nearly two years since I first gave my life to God. What an amazing time!

It has been awesome to trust God to guide me in the right direction and to lead me to people and situations that keep me from giving in to temptation.

When I first started my new life in God, I was so fearful that someone would come along who knew me only as that old drinking, gambling, porn-addicted guy I used to be—and either try to pull me back into that lifestyle or mock me for my new ways. In fact, for a long time I did my best to avoid conversations with those people. Or, if I had to talk to them, I'd keep my spiritual life a secret. It wasn't long, though, before I realized that tactic wasn't going to work.

I can vividly remember the night I begged God to provide me the strength to stand up for my newfound passion for him. I asked him to take me out of my comfort zone and to acknowledge my past indiscretions as well as the new life he'd given me. Before I knew it, he was using me to talk to and help people who were just like I used to be. I really felt like God allowed me to throw away the key to my past and to no longer fear my new relationship with him.

Obviously, I will never forget the struggles I went through and put my family and friends through. But I'm no longer ashamed or embarrassed by those incidents, because I know God has been shaping my life for a long time now. And that he wants me to be excited about my new life.

Ben

Over the last couple years, Ben has learned what Paul learned almost two thousand years ago: If anyone is in Christ, the new creation has come: The old has gone, the new is here! (2 Cor. 5:17 NIV). That's who Ben is these days—a new creation.

THAT'S NOT WHO YOU ARE ANYMORE!

I'm a basketball junkie. I grew up in Kentucky, where there was a hoop in every driveway. And we used those hoops as we all played and dreamed of one day becoming a Wildcat, then going on to stardom in the NBA. Even after going on to *mediocrity* at the *YMCA*, I remained passionate about the game. I coached my kids until they got to high school, I love March Madness, and I TiVo every NBA playoff game.

When I moved to Chicago, I turned that excitement toward the Bulls. I was a big Bulls fan when Michael Jordan ruled the NBA, and now I'm learning to love the young new Bulls. I was so pumped up when they acquired four-time defensive player of the year Ben Wallace from the Detroit Pistons. What a man! What a tremendous athlete and intimidating presence on the court!

I'll bet, though, that the transition may have been a little tough for Ben. After all, he'd been a Detroit

Piston his entire NBA career. He probably could have driven blindfolded to the Palace in Auburn Hills. He knew the shortcuts, the traffic patterns, and the places to stop for something to eat. He knew the inner workings of the Pistons' organization and he had friends among his teammates. But an offer was extended and a transaction was made. And in that moment, he was no longer a Detroit Piston. He became a Chicago Bull.

Now say that the Bulls should end up playing the Pistons in the Eastern Conference finals. What would happen if Big Ben, standing in the jump circle to tip off the game, began to think, "You know, I just don't feel like a Bull. I was a Piston for a long time, and I still feel like a Piston. I think I'll play for them tonight."

Well, no, that's not going to happen. No one's going to exchange his red and black uniform for the old blue and red combination. His new coach isn't going to suggest that he just go with his feelings and play for the Pistons in the first half and the Bulls in the second. The transaction took place. Ben's identity as a player completely and totally changed the instant he accepted the offer.

So he learned one step at a time how the Bulls do things. He memorized new plays, related to a new coach, started hanging out with a whole new set of teammates—even took on the challenge of navigating a new city. In short, he changed his mind and his mind-set to match the reality of his new identity.

I suspect there still may be days, as he pulls out of his driveway, that Ben Wallace feels like he should be heading to that old locker room back in Detroit. I'll bet you know what that kind of pull from the past feels like, too — and that you understand how easy it is for such feelings to help us find our way back to those old, sinful patterns. I mean, we've been there so many times, we can get there in the *dark*. And when that happens? Then God whispers, "But that's not *who you are*. Your identity changed." He doesn't even start with "You're not supposed to do that anymore." He goes straight to "That's not *who you are* anymore."

You see, a transaction took place between God the Father and you. An offer of grace was extended, and when you accepted it — in that instant you were rescued by the Son of God out of the kingdom of darkness and into the kingdom of light. Your identity changed; you are now a child of God. You're in a whole new place with a whole new life. You are a new creation. The old is gone and the new has come. That's who you *are*!

I'm constantly aware of God's continued coaching, telling me, "Come on, Mike, keep setting your mind on those things. Keep renewing your mind to that truth day after day after day." And I understand that if we don't do that—if we don't renew our minds to the truth of who we are in God's eyes day by day by day, we can start to believe we are the same old person. And once we believe that, we start to behave like that.

I ran into Ray the other day. He's a tough guy, with lots of leather and body art going on. He's been in all kinds of trouble in his life, most of it connected to drugs and alcohol. But then he accepted God's offer of a new start. He gave his life to Christ and was baptized in the lake at our church.

Ray told me he still has the picture of his baptism burned into his mind; that he envisions the "old guy" being buried and the "new guy" being raised up from the water grave. All of this is very new to him; he had never before done the church thing. But he's just a great guy, with a refreshing, honest faith.

A little ways into our conversation, Ray said, "I gotta tell you, Mike, that I relapsed the other day. I've been sober for a while now, but I started feeling a lot of stress about this relationship I'm in, and I relapsed. The strange thing was that I got mad at myself because *that's just not who I am anymore.* It felt weird, like it doesn't match up with who I am now. I'm not that old guy anymore."

I was amazed at his insight. I told him that even though it's sometimes three steps forward and two steps back, that still leaves him one step ahead. I shared 1 John 1:9 (my journal verse) with him, and we talked about God's unfailing grace. I said, "Man, you've been walking a certain way for a lot of years. You've had the same habits, the same patterns, the same way of reacting to problems for such a long time, you need to learn a new way of thinking. When we come to Christ and accept his forgiveness, he wipes our sins away. But there is no magic delete button in our heads. So we will still wrestle with the old stuff until we start changing the way we think."

I went on to tell him about my brother-in-law, Dave, who has a seventy-five-acre farm down in Kentucky. Dave has this path that runs from his barn down to one of his fields, and he could put his tractor on that path, close his eyes, and take his hands off the wheel, and that tractor would go to that field all on its own. You know why? Because Dave's tractor tires have dug deep ruts along the way—ruts created by traveling that same ole path every single day.

Some of us have been headed down the same ole paths for a very long time, which has, in effect, dug some pretty serious ruts in our minds. There is a lot of wisdom in the Sister Hazel song that goes,

> *If you want to be somebody else,*
> *If you're tired of fighting battles with yourself*
> *If you want to be somebody else*
> *Change your mind.*

In other words, create some new ruts to drive in.

OUR JOB IN WALKING FREE

Being saved and set free is a gift. But *walking* free? Now that's a choice—and one we have to make every single day. That's why Paul wrote, "Do not conform any longer to the pattern of this world [don't fall into the same old ruts], but be transformed by the renewing of your mind" (Rom. 12:2 NIV).

Paul is asking you to put yourself on a new path, to replace old lies with new truth, and to consciously develop new patterns of thinking. That old path you used to take—and those old ruts that used to define who you are—need to be filled in and repaved. The Holy Spirit of God will transform us; he alone has the power to pull that off. But it's clear we are to step up to our responsibilities as well. And the Bible gives us clear direction about what those responsibilities need to include.

Being saved and set free is a gift.
But *walking* free?
Now that's a choice —
and one we have to make
every single day.

Take the following two passages from Paul to the new believers at the church in Colosse. First, he says:

And now, just as you accepted Christ Jesus as your Lord, you must continue to live in obedience to him. Let your roots grow down into him and draw up nourishment from him, so you will grow in faith, strong and vigorous in the truth you were taught. Let your lives overflow with thanksgiving for all he has done. (Colossians 2:6–7)

Then he follows that advice with this:

Let the words of Christ, in all their richness, live in your hearts and make you wise. Use his words to teach and counsel each other. Sing psalms and hymns and spiritual songs to God with thankful hearts. And

*whatever you do or say, let it be as a representative of
the Lord Jesus, all the while giving thanks through him
to God the Father. (Colossians 3:16–17)*

Notice the active verbs Paul uses: *continue, live,
let, grow, use, counsel,* and more. These are things *we*
can do every day; actions we must take to help us
renew our minds and establish new patterns. You
and I are responsible for re-wallpapering our minds.

Some people assume that God will do all that *for*
us, but that is not what the Bible says. God does not
make your roots go down deep into his marvelous
love *for* you. He will not sing psalms and hymns
and spiritual songs with thanksgiving in your heart
for you. He will not put on the full armor of God
for you. He will not take up your cross and deny
yourself *for* you. He will not renew your mind *for*
you. Yes, you cooperate with the power of the Holy
Spirit to transform your life—but it's up to *you* to
renew your mind.

I want to encourage you to go back through this
book and highlight all the Scripture references.
Re-read them. Look them up in your Bible to better
understand their context. Reflect and meditate on
them. Start to memorize the ones with particular
applicability to your life.

I do that. I write down Scriptures on index cards
and then, while I'm sitting in Chicago traffic (Ben

Wallace is not the only one who had to get used to
that!), I've got plenty of time to pull those cards
out and memorize them. Whatever it takes to get
the Truth in your mind and heart, start to do that.
You'll be amazed how it will change you.

I was first challenged to memorize Scripture when
I realized, that although I knew all the stats for my
favorite teams, and I could usually cruise through
the first round of *Jeopardy*, I didn't know what God
said about himself. I didn't know what God said
about me. I didn't know what God said
about the way he wanted me to live. So
I started memorizing this good, vital,
eternal information. And I found out Jesus
was right. The Truth—when you know it;
when you grasp it—really does set you free.

And that freedom can manifest itself in a myriad
of ways. Why should I ever say "I can't" when
Philippians 4:13 tells me I can do all things through
Christ who gives me strength? Why should I ever
be afraid when 2 Timothy 1:7 says that God did not
give me a spirit of fear, but he gave me one of power
and love and self-discipline? Why should I worry
and stress out all the time when 1 Peter 5:7 says I
can cast all my anxiety upon God because he cares
for me?

And that's only the beginning. Why should I
feel condemned when Romans 8:1 tells me there

is no condemnation to those who are in Christ Jesus? Why should I feel alone when God tells me in Hebrews 13:5, "I will never fail you. I will never forsake you"? Why should I feel like a loser when Romans 8:37 tells me I am more than a conqueror through him who loves me? And why should I let Satan, the thief, hack into my life and steal my identity when 1 John 4:4 tells me, "The Spirit who lives in you is greater than the spirit who lives in the world"?

As I redirect my mind to those truths and more, grasping how deep and how high and how long and how wide the love of God is for me, guess what starts to happen. My behavior starts to match up with my new identity. And I begin to live the kind of life God always wanted me to live.

BECOMING

Remember that little Tupperware ball that helped launch us into this whole discussion? We talked about how hard we try to fit these square pegs into the round hole—the God-shaped hole—in our heart. You have no idea how many things I have tried to cram into my life that have only left me frustrated and empty. Well, on second thought, maybe you do have an idea. Because maybe you have done the same.

It's true, though, that deep within our hearts resides a God-shaped hole, a perfect fit for Jesus in every way. No heart is too big, no heart is too small. Jesus is the answer; he fits them all. And do you remember, too, how you get Jesus into your heart? Do you recall that equation from John 1:12 that says Believe + Receive = Become (but to all who *believed* him and *received* him, he gave the right to *become* children of God)?

If you haven't already taken that step, you can "become" right now. Is it possible that God's been stirring in your heart and you're feeling some hope and some grace? Might you be thinking, "Maybe I could start over. Maybe I could hand God *my* Etch A Sketch life and let him erase it for me. Maybe I could walk free from my past and start to really live"?

Well, yes you can. If you simply *believe* in Jesus Christ, the only Son of God who came to this earth and died on a cross to cover all your sin. Who was buried and rose from the grave to give you eternal life in heaven. If you *receive* the grace that he's offering you, a transaction will be made. And you will *become* a child of God—which is, after all, your true identity.

Then, instead of jumping from relationship to relationship, attempting to find unfailing love, you will rest in the truth that Jesus Christ is the only one who can complete you. As you grow closer to him, grasping his high, wide, long, deep love for you, you will actually start bringing a better you into all your relationships.

Instead of letting some cover model become your role model, you will look in the mirror every day and say, "Check it out. I am fearfully and wonderfully made!" And when you talk to God, you'll say, "Thanks, God, for making me *me*. I am honored to be a temple that you want to live in, so I'm going to take care of this body. I'm not going to obsess about the externals, though, because I want to look good from the inside out." And you will.

Instead of chasing the American Dream and running so fast to prove to everyone that you're *somebody*, you will relax in the truth that you already are somebody in God's eyes. You won't need the applause of others, because you've already got the applause of the One who matters most. You will surrender control of your life and your career and watch as God stuffs your portfolio with such assets as love, joy, peace, patience, kindness, gentleness, faithfulness, and self-control.

And instead of staying locked up in the prison of your past, you will allow God to set you free. You will walk step by step with him every day, trusting in his power and his grace as you work to renew your mind and accepting the challenge of repaving the ruts along the path of your former life.

Yes, it's a whole new way of thinking. A whole new way of living. It's an identity that is rock solid and true. And it's who you can be forever.

IDENTITY RESTORED

My friends at Freedom in Christ Ministries compiled the list that follows, which I keep on my desk (not far from the Tupperware ball on my shelf) so I can see it every day. I would invite you to grab a copy of God's Word and read these Scriptures for yourself. Read them again and again—maybe even memorize some of them—so you can truly *grasp* them. So you can let the truth of what God says about you wash over you every single day.

Because I Am in Christ and Christ Is in Me ... I Am *Completely Accepted.*

God says ...

I am God's child.
John 1:12

I am Christ's friend.
John 15:15

I have been justified.
Romans 5:1

I am united with the Lord and I am one spirit with him.
1 Corinthians 6:17

I have been bought with a price; I belong to God.
1 Corinthians 6:19–20

I am a member of Christ's body.
1 Corinthians 12:27

I have been adopted as God's child.
Ephesians 1:5

I have direct access to God through the Holy Spirit.
Ephesians 2:18

I have been redeemed and forgiven of all my sins.
Colossians 1:14

I am complete in Christ.
Colossians 2:10

Because I Am in Christ and Christ Is in Me ... I Am *Totally Secure.*

God says ...

I am free forever from condemnation.
Romans 8:1–2

I am assured that God works all things together for good.
Romans 8:28

I cannot be separated from the love of God.
Romans 8:35–39

I have been established, anointed, and sealed by God.
2 Corinthians 1:21–22

I am confident that God will finish the good work he started in me.
Philippians 1:6

I am a citizen of heaven.
Philippians 3:20

I am hidden with Christ.
Colossians 3:3

I have not been given a spirit of fear, but of power, love and self discipline.
2 Timothy 1:7

I can find mercy and grace to help in time of need.
Hebrews 4:16

I am born of God and the evil one cannot touch me.
1 John 5:18

Because I Am in Christ and Christ Is in Me ... I Am *Deeply Significant.*

God says ...

I am the salt of the earth and the light of the world.
Matthew 5:13 – 14

*I am a branch of the true vine, Jesus,
a channel of his life.*
John 15:5

I have been chosen to bear fruit.
John 15:16

I am a personal, Spirit-empowered witness of Christ.
Acts 1:8

I am a temple of God.
1 Corinthians 3:16

I am a minister of reconciliation for God.
2 Corinthians 5:17 – 21

I am God's co-worker.
2 Corinthians 6:1

I am seated with Christ in the heavenly realm.
Ephesians 2:6

I am God's workmanship, created for good works.
Ephesians 2:10

I may approach God with freedom and confidence.
Ephesians 3:12

I can do all things through Christ who strengthens me.
Philippians 4:13

SONG CREDITS

Willow Creek Association
Vision, Training, Resources for Prevailing Churches

This resource was created to serve you and to help you build a local church that prevails. It is just one of many ministry tools that are part of the Willow Creek Resources® line, published by the Willow Creek Association together with Zondervan.

The Willow Creek Association (WCA) was created in 1992 to serve a rapidly growing number of churches from across the denominational spectrum that are committed to helping unchurched people become fully devoted followers of Christ. Membership in the WCA now numbers over 12,000 Member Churches worldwide from more than ninety denominations.

The Willow Creek Association links like-minded Christian leaders with each other and with strategic vision, training, and resources in order to help them build prevailing churches designed to reach their redemptive potential. Here are some of the ways the WCA does that.

- **The Leadership Summit**—a once a year, two-and-a-half-day conference to envision and equip Christians with leadership gifts and responsibilities. Presented live at Willow Creek as well as via satellite broadcast to over 130 locations across North America, this event is designed to increase the leadership effectiveness of pastors, ministry staff, volunteer church leaders, and Christians in the marketplace.

- **Ministry-Specific Conferences** — throughout each year the WCA hosts a variety of conferences and training events — both at Willow Creek's main campus and offsite, across the U.S., and around the world — targeting church leaders and volunteers in ministry-specific areas such as: small groups, preaching and teaching, the arts, children, students, volunteers, stewardship, etc.

- **Willow Creek Resources®** — provides churches with trusted and field-tested ministry resources in such areas as leadership, evangelism, spiritual formation, spiritual gifts, small groups, stewardship, student ministry, children's ministry, the use of the arts — drama, media, contemporary music — and more.

- **WCA Member Benefits** — includes substantial discounts to WCA training events, a 20 percent discount on all Willow Creek Resources®, *Defining Moments* monthly audio journal for leaders, quarterly *Willow* magazine, access to a Members-Only section on WillowNet, monthly communications, and more. Member Churches also receive special discounts and premier services through WCA's growing number of ministry partners — Select Service Providers — and save an average of $500 annually depending on the level of engagement.

For specific information about WCA conferences, resources, membership, and other ministry services contact:

Willow Creek Association
P.O. Box 3188
Barrington, IL 60011-3188
Phone: 847-570-9812
Fax: 847-765-5046
www.willowcreek.com

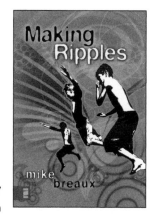

Making Ripples

Mike Breaux

Mike Breaux doesn't do life halfway —maybe that's why he thinks a "cannonball" is the only suitable entry into a swimming pool. "Deep down, I think all of us sense we were put on this planet to do something significant—to touch someone's life; to do some good." Again and again, he's seen the cannonball approach make that happen. "Water goes flying everywhere! The ripples go out, hit the side, and come back in." In this book, Breaux shares the concept of creating "ripples"—where a life touches a life, which touches a life, which touches a life.

Hardcover, Jacketed 0-310-27253-X

Pick up a copy today at your favorite bookstore!